D0985268

SOURCES OF CULTURAL ESTRANGEMENT

STUDIES IN THE SOCIAL SCIENCES

edited by C.A.O. van Nieuwenhuijze

7

SOURCES OF CULTURAL ESTRANGEMENT

by

DERIC REGIN

KLINCK MEMORIAL LIBRARY
Concordia Teachers College
River Forest, Illinois 60305

1969

MOUTON

THE HAGUE · PARIS

© Copyright 1969 in The Netherlands.
Mouton & Co. N.V., Publishers, The Hague.

No part of this book may be translated or reproduced in any form, by print, photoprint, microfilm, or any other means, without written permission from the publishers.

LIBRARY OF CONGRESS CATALOG CARD NUMBER: 71-85899

Printed in The Netherlands by Mouton & Co., Printers, The Hague.

98501

ARGUMENT

This inquiry aims at re-evaluating a concept about which much has been written recently and which through misuse has acquired an unfortunate and misleading glamor. The author hopes that by placing the notion in its proper perspective some of the confusion surrounding the idea of alienation may be cleared away.

In the following pages the problem of human estrangement will be put in its original context, and be seen within the cultural development of the last two centuries. Thus it is not a sociological study of symptomatic group unrest, but foremost an effort to trace the growth of modern man's consciousness of himself and of his outside world as separate entities.

Since this work evaluates the totality of a historical experience, the concept of culture and cultural history will be considered first in order to establish a proper footing. Following this the notion of alienation (again as a total and historical experience) can be viewed in its cultural setting. I shall try to make clear what cultural estrangement is NOT, briefly review a number of its confusing varieties, and focus it on the awareness of human freedom.

My next task will be to analyze modern culture as a human product, whose two generating factors are the activities of play and of labor. Consequently in the second chapter play and labor will be discussed in their historical role. With this we are clearly in the field of social communication, a notion which will be further elaborated in the next section, where it is linked with the inevitable relationship between individual and masses – the focusing point of modern cultural history.

With the theoretical analysis out of the way, we can then in the fourth chapter turn to a survey of the thoughts on cultural estrangement propounded by the major nineteenth-century authors, thereby distinguishing subsequent phases of historical development. Finally, I shall try to summarize the materials discussed by suggesting that the sources of alienation as found in the awareness of culture, play, labor, individual, collective, communication or eschatology, are in their deepest sense related to the decisive crisis of the eighteenth century: the era of political, industrial and Romanticist revolutions.

I am indebted to Benjamin Hunningher of Amsterdam University, who was the first to know about this project and to encourage me to put it into shape. I am especially grateful to Elizabeth Vermey of Bryn Mawr, who has read the whole manuscript and whose sense of logic has been highly beneficial for the exposition of the philosophical themes. Karl Löwith of Heidelberg, expert on alienation, gave me his kind advice on this matter.

I wish to thank Johan Hollak of Amsterdam University who, specialist in Hegelian and Marxist thought, has provided me with many helpful suggestions as well as corrections. I further owe a debt to Henry Shapiro of Riverside, California, and to Eva Keuls of Emory, who have read parts of the work.

Nancy Farrand Regin, as always, has been my indispensable editor.

CONTENTS

Argument   5

Introduction   9
   1. The Fruits and the Flowers   9
   2. The Counter-point of History 14
   3. The Classical Synthesis 21

  I. The Historical Concept of Alienation 24
   1. Awareness, Human and Historical 24
   2. Estrangement, its Versions and Varieties 31
   3. Freedom, its Opportunity and Unfulfillment 41

 II. Labor, Play, Culture 49
   1. Man and Work 50
   2. Man and Play 59
   3. Man and Culture 65

III. Communication and the Masses 73
   1. The Price of Communication 73
   2. Individual and Collective 77

IV. Survey of Nineteenth-Century Thought About Cultural
   Estrangement 88
   1. Beginnings: Schiller, Fichte, Schelling 88
   2. Establishment: Hegel, Goethe, Wagner 96
   3. Expansion: Kierkegaard, Marx, Nietzsche 109
   4. United States: Emerson, Thoreau, Melville 121
   5. Eschatological Overtones 134

Conclusion 147

INTRODUCTION

1. THE FRUITS AND THE FLOWERS

Culture is the test of a society. The historical significance of nations and groups of peoples united in civilizations is recognized in their fruition. The history of ancient China is lost for all but the specialist, but its achievements in arts and letters are still public domain. When the political and institutional history of Greece has faded away in the background, Homer, Pindar, Plato, or Thucydides will remain to instruct and counsel us.

With this we are already in the middle of a crucial problem. For the use of the word culture here suggests superficially an aggregate of brilliant achievements, but its real meaning lies far deeper and implies maturation. The fruits of society are great when gathered in the museums, but their most important phase is one of suffering and ripening, and that, as Rilke says, means "toiling in obscurity".[1]

The misunderstandings about human estrangement so rampant in today's popular magazines and books, can often be traced to a tendency to treat forms of alienation detached from their cultural setting. In order to give ourselves a sound footing we must needs start with some basic questions about the meaning, structure and function of culture. The word is as elusive as it is alluring. Most definitions seem to raise more questions than they answer, and instead of narrowing its content, describe the term in such a diffuse and confused manner, that one hesitates to mention it at all.

The notion of culture in the nineteenth century grows in significance with man's increased consciousness of himself and his history. During this period it also undergoes striking changes in its meaning. Originally derived from the Latin *cultura*, the care of the land, agriculture in general, it comes soon also to be known as the development of human

---

[1] "Im Saal", *Sämtliche Werke*, I, 521.

training. Later culture becomes a state of intellectual progress or, especially with Matthew Arnold, the "distinterested endeavour after man's perfection".[2] Various particular meanings are added to the word. It can indicate the general scope of arts and letters, society as a whole, a way of life in all its physical and intellectual aspects. The semantic development of the word culture is interesting inasmuch as it explains something about the thinking on artistic, political and economic changes in the nineteenth and twentieth century, and it may in itself be seen "as a special kind of map by means of which the nature of the changes can be explored".[3]

The diffusion in the meaning of culture necessarily leads to a vague and loose usage of the word. It is often used as a substitute for society, and anthropologists especially in their attempt to treat man as a scientific object, have frequently confused his social being with his cultural expressions.[4] Culture is NOT society. It is a product of society. It is that by which the vitality of a society spreads, propagates, and is remembered in history.

Under these confused circumstances it is understandable that the need has been felt to create order in the chaos, and since culture cannot be claimed exclusively by any one specialist, poets, psychiatrists, historians, biologists, philosophers, anthropologists can all from their specific point of view try for a definition. One is finally relieved when one comes across the simple statement that "culture is always synthesis",[5] but brevity is no substitute for information. T. S. Eliot, after carefully charting his way towards a definition, produces the idea that culture may be simply described "as that which makes life worth living".[6] On this he bases the theory that culture and Christianity must go hand in hand, a doctrine brightly attractive to modern clergymen, but one, we must assume, with which Christ would have found it hard to cope. More soundly and scholarly reasoned is Emil Brunner's scepticism about the possibilities of a socalled 'Christian' culture; he merely stresses that culture is the "formation of human life which has its origin not in mere biological necessity, but in spiritual impulsion".[7]

[2] M. Arnold, *Culture and Anarchy* (New York, 1928), 25.
[3] Raymond Williams, *Culture and Society*, 1780-1950 (Garden City, 1960), xiv.
[4] See J. Barzun, *Science: the Glorious Entertainment* (New York, 1964), 9/10.
[5] G. Simmel, *Philosophische Kultur* (Potsdam, 3rd ed., 1923), 249.
[6] T. S. Eliot, *Notes towards the Definition of Culture* (New York, 1949), 26. Similarly relaxed is Baldwin's definition in *Dictionary of Philosophy and Psychology*: "Culture is whatever affects the intellectual status of man."
[7] E. Brunner, *Christianity and Civilization* (London, 1949), II, 128.

It must at least be clear that culture is thoroughly human. Animals may live in a society – they produce no culture. They may baffle us with brilliant achievements, honeycombs, beaverdams – they have no culture. Some can acquire skills by imitation and training, yet neither will these mount up to cultural expressions.[8] It is only man's reflecting consciousness which molds and preserves a lasting imprint of his work. It is for this reason that a conception of civilization as being a cornucopia of diverse mental efforts to adorn society has little real value. It is understandable that a nation like ours, blessed with natural and material abundance throughout its history, is easily inclined to extend the idea of 'plenty' to cultural acquisition. But culture is not a commodity. Nor is it 'archaeological bric-a-brac', as Lamprecht rightly asserts, although he hastens to add that no one can be prevented from clinging to this definition.[9]

Though culture is not merely a cornucopia, its fruits obviously can be enjoyed. A distinction simply has to be made between its picking-time and its ripening, between harvest and maturation. Cultural expressions can be no more constructed and designed than the cones on a hemlock. They emerge organically if circumstances are cooperative. Frobenius, studying the societies of Africa, comes to the conclusion that culture is not made by man, but that it throbs through man (*durchleben*). He prefers to replace the word culture with the Greek *Paideuma* to indicate the autonomy under which it grows, matures and declines. Thus it develops through a life-cycle from intuitive infancy through idealistic adolescence and the mechanical adult world of facts, until it becomes senile in its final inorganic state.[10] This reasoning is based on the Vitalist morphology of which Oswald Spengler is the greatest representative and which is, to say the least, debatable. Leaving, however, the cyclical speculations aside, one can agree that the distinction of culture as a force is a helpful way of avoiding the one-sided horn-of-plenty conception.

It would appear that culture obtains its peculiar depth from the fact that it is both function and product, maturation and fruition, and that these two phases cannot be separated one from the other without doing injustice to the full dimensions of culture. Nor should it be thought that

---

[8] This contradicts T. Dobzhansky's statement that "culture is acquired by imitation, training and learning", *Mankind evolving* (New Haven, 1962), 8. However, from the context it is clear that he means these to be human activities.
[9] K. Lamprecht, "Was ist Kulturgeschichte?", *Deutsche Zeitschrift für Geschichtswissenschaft*, I (1896/7), 154.
[10] L. Frobenius, *Paideuma* (München, 1921), 58.

while culture can be said to grow organically it does not need mechanical means to fulfill itself. Culture is the care for nature, but also its disciplining. With ingenuity and skill man not only grows bigger and better potatoes, but can also train infants to become reading and writing children. Man's deliberate harnessing and changing of nature renders it serviceable to him.[11] Bees and beavers are able to subdue and change nature in an efficient as well as beautiful manner, and so are other animals. But man alone has the choice of doing it in this or that manner and of inventing varieties. He is free to change his technique, to invent new tools, and to develop new styles. The essential nature of culture is its freedom.

The freedom lies in the expression. The building of a house is relatively speaking no greater a feat than the construction of a hornets' nest. But the varieties of material, ornaments and styles, that which constitutes the quality of architecture, are the workings of a free expression. Expression implies the turning of something inside out. Something private, something unconscious, is publicized. It is submitted to the public consciousness.[12] The sculptor's statue may technically be a portrayal, or the representation of an animal or an object; artistically speaking, however, it is an expression which betrays the maker's private freedom. The choice of the material, the texture, the general rendering, is authentically his own. It reveals his unconscious privacy. It is this element which is preserved in culture. We do not have to confine ourselves to those activities recognized as purely artistic. Everything serving society and undergoing changes in the history of society can be part of the cultural expression. The historical fashions of our garments succeed one another according to inward needs and become public style. Similarly the designs of cutlery, glasswork or pottery characterize the different tastes and preferences of distinct periods.

Culture thus embraces a wide variety of activities which leave their mark upon history. The activities themselves are not culture, but become so in the awareness of historical change. Some of the expressions are longer and better remembered than others and this causes us, rightly or wrongly, to speak of high and low culture. It is clear that the Italian civilization will be longer remembered for its Leonardos than for its

[11] E. Bernheim, *Lehrbuch der historischen Methode* (München, 1914), 60. Cf. F. Jodle, who points to the elements of human struggle with nature, *Die Kulturgeschichtsschreibung* (Halle, 1887), 112, and Paul Barth, *Die Philosophie der Geschichte als Soziologie* (Leipzig, 4th ed., 1921), 602/3.
[12] Cf. Eisler's *Wörterbuch der philosophischen Begriffe*: "Culture is the bringing out and elaboration (*Herausarbeitung*) of potentialities."

Lancias. To rate cultural achievements in terms of more and better is relatively immaterial here and can only be undertaken with some chance of success in the specialized fields of say, the history of art, of music, of architecture of literature, or of philosophy. But no one would deny of course that there exist grades and levels of intensity. The expressions of Greek and European drama, for instance, cannot be proved to be historically more important than the Roman aqueducts or the invention of the telephone. They are simply of a different order. But these dramatic forms do reveal more about the deeply brooding privacy of mankind at specific eras in history. They convey suffering. And so that which is often remembered best and longest in the history of culture roots in the tragic suffering as expressed in poetic and artistic communications.

What we are dealing with here is less such human experiences as injustice, deprivation, discrimination, famine, pauperism and others which constitute the accidental suffering of many at all times. The tragic lies in the experience that this suffering is also existential, that it is inherent in man inasmuch as he faces inexorable absolutes. Many people are ignorant of this experience, others just to do not bother to reflect on it. But poets and philosophers do. They deal with the heroic suffering best indicated by the Greek word *pathos*, which as well as suffering includes passion and wisdom. The intensity of pathos results in the most deeply moving configurations of culture. They can be as different as Prometheus, Don Quixote, and Faust, but they all represent the universality of individual suffering. Tragic culture is not a specific variety of civilization. It represents the ordinary and humanly normal in its most intense and most universal form.

It is for this reason that the artistic, metaphysical and religious expressions of culture have often been considered more demonstrative of a particular epochal style and what this existentially represents, (the contents of human hopes, dreams, sufferings) than political institutions or social customs. One ought to add, though, that this fact is by no means an absolute standard and can cogently be ignored by those who do not see and accept such metaphysical dimensions as 'tragic pathos' or 'existential sufferings'. There is no reason why the notion of culture should be forced into a doctrinaire formula. Since it is an expression of life itself, spontaneous and vibrant, it does not brook the assumptions of a definition.

Avoiding this we can reiterate the foregoing and juxtapose the most striking attributes of culture in its fullest sense. We have seen that it is thoroughly human. As such some scholars have with varying degree of persuasiveness subjected it to the divisions of human ages. It is organically conceived and governments, for political or nationalistic reasons, trying to establish it by decree will fail in the effort. Thirdly, culture is understood as both a process of maturation and the product of this process, that is as customs, inventions, institutions, arts, philosophy. It demands disciplinary training, though its essence is freedom. Finally, it is a symbolic expression rooted in a pre-conscious privacy and publicized for the common consciousness where it is preserved and extended through history.

The chaotic situation in which contemporary culture seems to find itself has led some authors to distinguish it as a late historical phase which they call civilization. Spengler used the term in this sense and points to the megalopolitan character in contrast to that of culture which is typified by the landscape. Tönnies divides culture and civilization according to the prevalence of either agriculture or industry,[13] and others, less concerned about the chronological division, stress the control over nature in culture against that over man himself in civilization.[14] In general, however, the words are constantly interchanged, and in this investigation they will also be used indiscriminately.

Whether or not our civilization is dying is not relevant to us here. To study the extent of estrangement it is more important to know from what norm culture is estranged. What is the norm? If culture indeed is a synthesis, could alienation perhaps mean the disturbance of this synthesis? In order to answer this one first has to examine what are the forces synthesized in culture.

2. THE COUNTER-POINT OF HISTORY

It is doubtful that in this age of specialization one can make the statement that cultural history is a kind of superbranch and represents the "core of all history and the key to its inner understanding".[15] Many historians will dismiss this as emotional subjectivism and themselves rather regard cultural and intellectual history as one among many equally valid approaches to the past. The cultural historian cannot

---

[13] F. Tönnies, *Gemeinschaft und Gesellschaft* (Darmstadt, 1963, 8th ed.), 243.
[14] E. Bernheim, *op. cit.*, 60.
[15] H. Schaller, *Die Europäische Kulturphilosophie* (München, 1940), 109. Nor can one say that all history is cultural as does M. Mandelbaum, *The Problem of Historical Knowledge* (New York, 1938), 292.

claim priority rights, nor does he enjoy special prerogatives. But, though his method is by no means better, more accurate, or more persuasive than others, there is no denying that it is entirely different from that of economic, political or institutional historians. It is obviously not the place here to enter into a discussion on the technical problems of historiography. But if one sets out to study the process of alienation as a basic element of modern civilization, a few words must be devoted to the unique objectives of cultural history.

The cultural historian differs from his colleagues in that he does not study facts, but expressions. He is not interested in the human actions, the *res gestae* of the past, but primarily in human communications. His concern is not so much with what people do or have, as with what they are. The latter they leave hidden in a number of symbolic configurations, the doctrines of religion, the codes of law, or the works of literature, which are the real documents of the cultural historian. Macaulay devotes numerous pages to the confused and detailed parliamentary debates about the various toleration bills proposed after the Glorious Revolution.[16] The cultural historian on the other hand, will consider Locke's letters concerning toleration as the epitome of the growing consciousness of tolerance in the consensus of the time. Unlike the political theorist he does not treat them as individual doctrine, but as a symbolic expression of historical change. Nor does he describe the colors and composition of works of art for their esthetic evaluation, as does the art historian; rather he tries to find out what they tell us about the tastes, thoughts and ideals of the contemporary man. He has no need to analyze in detail Wordsworth's *Prelude*, like the literary critic; to him it reveals the new reaching out and new apprehensions in a time of political and industrial movement. The cultural historian is constantly engaged in the discipline of transmuting situations of specific fields into historical situations. He is fundamentally a translator. As such he knows the dangers involved in rearranging the logic of one system into another, and he is aware of the inevitable inadequacies of this performance. To put Hegel's dialectic, Manet's Impressionism, or Wedekind's early Expressionism in a historcal perspective is a transaction which rarely succeeds without sacrificing some overtones here and some values there. Thus he becomes highly suspect to the specialist. And this the more so, since he is primarily a synthesizer, groping his way towards unifying statements. He draws freely from the professional monographs, leaving out those details which he does not regard as

[16] Macaulay, *History of England*, III, xi.

typical. In fact, whereas the specialist is careful to include as many
pertinent data as he can collect, the cultural historian seems to thrive
on the act of omission. It is self-evident that such a procedure can
easily result in sweeping judgments and amateurish treatment of details.
The only manner by which the cultural historian can guard himself
against these dangers is to equip himself with a thorough knowledge of
the purely historical events of a given period, and an inside technical
knowledge of at least some of the specific fields involved in his broad
survey. Cultural history is distinct from its sister branches, as Huizinga
indicates, in that it concentrates on deeper, general themes. "The details
of cultural history belong to the realm of morals, customs, folklore,
antiquities, and easily degenerate into curios." [17]

Here Huizinga follows Burckhardt who, of all cultural historians, is
the most formidable in penetrating through a jumble of conflicting and
confusing details to the essential stirrings of a civilisation. "History is
chaos", Charles Beard remarks, "and every attempt to interpret it otherwise is an illusion." [18] Yet, though one should not fondle any hope of
creating a lasting order, the effort can be made to sort out main forces
from by-products. Burckhardt's introduction to his work on Ancient
Greece is a classical statement on the advantages of cultural history.
The task he sets himself is to give the history of the Greek ways of
thinking and perceiving (*Anschauung*) and to strive for a knowledge of
the vital FORCES, constructive as well as destructive, operating in Greek
life.[19] His entire investigation is directed towards the 'history of the
Greek spirit", and he sees the main advantage of cultural history in the
certitude of its conception which it derives from what sources supply
in a neutral, undeliberate, unbiased way. It aims not so much at a detailed narrative as at the TYPICAL of the many aspects. It penetrates to
the inner realm of man in the past, and "declares what he was, wanted,
thought, perceived and was capable of".[20] Here the general data are
more important than the specific, the recurring more significant than
the isolated (*einmalig*) facts.

While Ranke is the consummate virtuoso of the detail, Burckhardt is

[17] J. Huizinga, *Verzamelde Werken*, VII, 47. English translation in *Man and Ideas* (New York, 1959), 28.
[18] Charles A. Beard, "Written History as an Act of Faith", in *The Philosophy of History in our Time*, ed. Hans Meyerhoff (Garden City, 1959), 151. See for the vain search for unity in history: Frederick J. Teggart, *Theory and Processes of History* (Berkeley, Cal., 1941), 40-50, and K. Jaspers, *The Origin and Goal of History* (New Haven, 1953).
[19] J. Burckhardt, *Griechische Kulturgeschichte* (Leipzig, n.d.), I, 5.
[20] *Ibid.*, I, 6.

foremost the master of proportion and universal meaning. His search for the vital and essential leads him to unorthodox sources and with professional arrogance he taunts his colleagues with their so-called 'scientific' method and their ignorance of the fact that true historiography demands "living in that fine, spiritual *fluidum*" which comes from works of art and poetry just as much as from the archives.[21] But what are essentials? Although no one doubts Burckhardt's unique contributions, his conceptions of the Greek era and the Renaissance have been challenged and persuasively attacked. In our age when a pluralistic oulook defies any belief in unity and proportioned order, a serene and esthetic cultural history of Burckhardt's kind is no longer feasible. He himself was aware of the period of transition in which he lived, and in order to escape from the contemporary confusions and upheavals he withdrew into a sort of Stoic-Epicurian privacy.[22]

But we who must face the facts of alienation squarely can neither bury ourselves in the past, nor pretend that we can construct a framework of unity for our age. We are still being buffeted by the forces of our time. We are perplexed by contradictory facts, out of balance in the century's shift of power relationships. It would be naive and hazardous to try and present a historically developed picture of the essentials of our time. The essentials are still mostly hidden, and a matter of guesswork. Even if we think that we have a fairly accurate grasp of them, we must admit that we lack a reliable concept of relative proportion. Therefore any attempt at a cultural history of the modern age must be extremely careful in positing its guidelines. They can be only of a tentative nature, and are merely artificial tools for arriving at some illumination. The phenomena of alienation are clearly essential to us at this point, but in using them as the framework of a historical analysis it must be remembered that other tentative frameworks might serve as well. Moreover, in coming ages our concern about human estrangement may turn out to be of secondary importance and simply a passing spell of dizziness.

If we then are to use the concept of alienation as the *leitmotif* of modern cultural history, we must, it seems, be fully aware of the great change which has taken place in the structure of society, one which inevitably reflects on its cultural expressions. Burckhardt concentrates preferably on those eras of civilization in which a fairly harmonious

---

[21]   *Ibid.*, I, 9. Letter of April 17, 1847, in *Briefe Jacob Burckhardts an G. und J. Kinkel* (Basel, 1921), 142.
[22]   K. Löwith, *Meaning in History* (Chicago, 1949), 23.

balance may be said to prevail. But from the end of the eighteenth century on, an increasing questioning becomes apparent about the 'originality' of the individual over against the collective society.[23] This self-conscious thinking about the split between the individual and the species which starts with the Romanticists, and spreads through the nineteenth century to become known as alienation in our time, is basically the theme of this book. 'Individual' and 'collective', which are originally integrated entities in the play and freedom of society, have become separated notions in our consciousness. Accordingly, each has its own representative philosophy. Hegel can still envisage a realm in which they are reconciled as thesis and antithesis. But after him the unity breaks down into two separate movements: Existentialist thinking and Dialectic Materialism with their respective captains Kierkegaard and Marx. The division is similarly reflected in the theory which distinguished individual history (political) from collective history (cultural).[24] Individuality is pitched against group, initiative against conformity, creativity against mechanization.[25]

It is in this light, and placed in this perspective that modern history receives a double dimension. In general one can in important periods observe a characteristic structure which may be called the counter-point of history. Whereas popular history indulges in the surface tune of more or less glorious events, the professional account of the past must also include the counter-movements that run underneath the *cantus firmus*.

Thus the history of seventeenth-century Holland certainly is that of Orange's *Apologia*, Grotius' *De iure belli ac pacis*, Rembrandt's *Night Watch*, Spinoza's *Ethics*, Leeuwenhoek's microscope, and of de Ruyter, Hendrik de Keyser, Oldenbarneveldt, and Sweelinck; it is also that of the development of ruthless colonial exploitation, of murder and plunder in Java and in the Moluccas. Germany in the nineteenth century presents the world a fabulous array of genius in Goethe, Hegel, Beethoven, Brahms, Ranke, Helmholtz, Humboldt, Gauss, Wundt, Nietzsche, Bismarck, Marx and many others; it also cultivates the most morbid nationalism, which eventually is to lead to total disaster. The story of the United States will always be one of liberty and opportunity; yet few other nations in the grim annals of colonial history have with such

[23] It is for instance one of the leading themes in Schiller's work. See F. Meinecke, "Schiller und der Individualitätsgedanke", *Werke* (Stuttgart, 1959), VI.
[24] Lamprecht, *op. cit.*, 144.
[25] For the rift in the polarity of individual and community, see Jaspers, "Das Kollektiv und der Einzelne", *Philosophie und Welt* (München, 1958), 69.

radicality stamped out the last vestiges of indigenous life, or withheld
with such tenacity the liberty of their constitution from important groups
in the commonwealth. The counterpoint of history is a process of fugal
variations not unlike Bach's *Musical Offering*, except that there is no
final chord. At its best it can be suspended in the dissonance of the
Tragic. But that means the awareness of defeat. Our age cannot face
the idea of defeat. The tragic hero is absent.

Winston Churchill in his boys' book conception of history liked to
present his life as a victory over tyranny. But the counter-point spins
a long persistent tune of defeat. The old feudal and colonial order for
which he unashamedly stood he sees disintegrating during his time. The
triumphant V-sign in actuality signifies Victorian illusions. History must
record that he achieved precisely that which he feared most: the dissolution of the British Empire. If he, besides his obvious great gifts,
had had the gift of tragic greatness which an Oedipus, a Hamlet, a Faust
have in abundance, he would have recognized the defeat and vanity of
his efforts.

Some will insist on seeing historical irony in this situation. But irony
as Kierkegaard teaches us is an instant in which we recognize an absolute negation. History, in contrast, is the narration of a process, an
endless string of instants. Others, following Hegel, may call it the 'cun-
ning of Reason' which sacrifices personal passions and illusions for its
own realization.[26] But this implies the assumption that there exists an
absolute idea and purpose behind historical events, a conception which
few today are willing to accept. In our own time, for our own purpose,
it is more useful to realize how two dialectically related counter-
movements have provided us with an uncertain, inconclusive picture of
our historical situation.

What is the contrapuntal structure of the modern age? Starting with
the political, industrial and artistic revolutions of the late eighteenth
century, the obvious melodic line is ascending, untrammeled, and confident like a Verdi motif. We recognize the successive degrees of progress, emancipation, tolerance, understanding, expressing itself in new
constitutions, reform bills, political parties, labor unions and manifestos.
Why then, one is bound to ask, if the general auguries are so favorable
for a freer and more perfect society, do we see emerge an increasing
pessimism from Schopenhauer to Freud, and an insistent eschatological
prophecy from Hegel to Spengler? Why then the widening impact of a

---

[26]   Hegel, *Philosophie der Geschichte*, Einl., II, b.

philosophy of anxiety? Why the growing neurosis? Why the need for narcotics, sedatives, barbiturates? Never before, it seems, has there been an age in which the counter-point of trends was more dramatically displayed. On the one hand, there is the full realization of new liberties and opportunities, on the other, cultural unfulfilment and anxiety.[27]

Historical counter-point, however, is no mere mechanical fabrication. Behind it, in our time, stands the vital dilemma of the individual and the collective. How vital and decisive this dilemma is has been set forth by Jaspers in a lecture of 1956. Looking at the problem from our vantage-point, he relates it to the consciousness of a possible end of the world. That which Jesus and the early Christians "experienced wrongly", is now a technical possibility, and man's thinking is naturally under pressure of this threat. Jasper's conclusion is that all depends on the survival of the individual. Seeing how the uniqueness of the personality is more and more ossifying into a fixed pattern, which "abhors solitude, lives with open doors, knows no space for himself, is always available, always active and constantly bound by the Type", he fears that if this development goes beyond the point where the individual can survive, the end of the world may well be near in a few decades. Only man in his individual authority can hope to save mankind from perdition.[28]

Clearly Jaspers' view is part and parcel of Existentialist philosophy, and many who have set their hopes on the strength of the collective will inevitably doubt that the survival of our civilization is contingent upon the integrity of the individual. The main point for us, however, is the realization in the contemporary mind that the collective and the single are pitched against each other as decisive magnitudes, and that the fact of modern anxiety derives from this situation. It is disquieting that the cumulative effect of more and wider opportunities, far from satisfying our search for security, or peace of mind as the slogan runs, has brought us into a more and more acutely realized state of unfulfilment. It is no slight thing to become aware of the fact that with every new liberty obtained, a fraction of our individual independence has been bartered away.

The modern mind as a whole has accepted this price. It is not for us to judge the validity of this choice, nor to speculate on its consequences. Here we are merely engaged in a study of the cultural scope of the separation between self and community. Whereas classical culture demonstrates an integration and mutual identification of individual and

[27] Jaspers, *op. cit.*, 71.
[28] *Ibid.*, 75.

society, in our mind the two can no longer be reconciled in a forceful unity. Consequently the experience of the tragic escapes us. For tragedy is in individual suffering if this suffering is existential and humanly universal, and so to speak on behalf of mankind whose lot is epitomized in the awareness of the tragic protagonist. Oedipus' grief would be merely pathetic if it were caused by accident. But since it is lifted into the existential dimensions of absolute forces, controlling and threatening man, the common audience identifies itself with him: the general and the individual are integrated in a tragic experience. That which at the height of the Greek and European civilization is expressed as tragic awareness is merely a picture of the great conscious mind acknowledging defeat. Indeed the measure of classical symmetry is manifest in the harmonization of two relativities: glory and defeat.

3. THE CLASSICAL SYNTHESIS

What does this notion of the classical mean? Is it the standard seal of perfection? Is it the mirror to be held up against us to reveal our deteriorated state? Is it the inheritance of something of our own, yet no longer our own?

Goethe, who is very conscious of living at the end of the classical era, distinguishes it as one of wholesomeness. "The classical I call the healthy, the Romantic the sick." [29] The obvious trouble with this statement is its uselessness. Goethe's own poetry, his novels, and especially his *Faust* are strongly tinged with a Romantic wash. After Schiller points out Goethe's Romantic traits, the latter is willing to concede this point.[30] It is obviously untenable to identify ALL non-classical forms of art with sickness. Classical and non-Classical are artificial notions, useful for periodization and other descriptive tasks, but only helpful if used in full knowledge of their pedagogic limitations. The terms Classical and non-Classical as they will be used in the following pages are not designations of something valid and something not so valid, something good and something not so good, something glorious and something not so glorious.

[29] Eckermann, *Gespräche mit Goethe* (Wiesbaden, 1959), 253.
[30] March 21, 1830, *Ibid.*, 309. The year before Goethe had admitted that in the second part of *Faust* the Classical and Romantic styles had been combined. *Ibid.*, 286. Cf. also E. M. Butler, *The Tyranny of Greece over Germany* (New York, 1935).

The classical simply is the normal. How must we understand this
without involving ourselves in clumsy generalizations? What are the
norms of the normal? Cannot, for instance, any age claim its cultural
style to be normal? By what authority can one accept borderlines for
the normal and non-normal? The answer must be: by common experience. The retired worker enjoying the little chores of his slowed
existence cannot necessarily be called sick. Biologically he behaves
absolutely normally, within the restrictions of his age. Compared to his
prime, however, when the begetting and raising of children, and the
skill of his daily labor occupy his attention, his retirement can be said
to be a-normal. This is not sickness. It is limitation. From now on the
man lives and works outside the vital circuits of society.

The norms of the normal are never self-set. They are organically
developed. They live in the genes, so to speak. The norms of the classical
drama from Aeschylus to Ibsen, regardless of the changes in techniques,
rules, unities, lie uninterruptedly in the central position of the hero.
When the modern drama of the anti- and epic theatre starts to develop
around 1800, its deliberate touch of absurdism means the undermining
of the heroic ideal. This obviously does not immediately reflect on its
esthetic merits. As long as it finds its own audiences it is socially
justified. All one can say is that it has left the original circuits of
culture. It is decentralized. It has lost the ties with its original cultural
ideal and authority, be it religious or humanistic. It can satisfy a
thousand and one particular and limited needs, it is by no means necessarily sick, and can take part in the commercial boom. But it knows
no cultural norm. It can in self-defense bring in many theories to explain
its purpose. It is characteristically eclectic. But it knows no norm.

The classical, of course, has overtones of the ideal, the standard
module, or the 'robust' (tüchtig) as Goethe calls it, all of which are of
secondary importance to us.[31] What is immediately relevant though, is
its inner poise, the repose in its attitudes, which derive from the certitude
of ideals. We have declared ideals to be illusions. The validity of our
judgment is not under discussion. The historical fact can merely be
described. We must infer that with the abandoning of cultural illusion
we have lost our anchorage. Our relationships have become relative.

---

[31] The idea of the classical is derived from the *cives classici*, the first of the
various levels of citizens as classified by Servius Tullius (578-534), Grimm,
Deutsches Wörterbuch. Baldwin, *Dictionary of Philosophy and Psychology*, takes
the notion of classical for "conformity to such laws as clearness, truth, unity".
The romantic, in contrast, is the subjective.

Since we have lost our center, we have given up spatial relations and perspective in painting, dispensed with tonal keys in music, eliminated plot from novel and play, poetic coherence from poetry, legal principle from jurisprudence, resurrection and eternity from religion, a moral basis from political actions, a metaphysical Idea from philosophy, the Newtonian unity from our cosmology. We float in the infinite skies of opportunities. Our guides are the thrusts of chance and relativity.

Is it good, is it wrong? No one can tell. The answer lies in the historical future. At any rate the non-classical cannot simply be judged wrong on the exclusive ground that it does not adopt the classical norm. It is merely that the tight cohesion of individual and species becomes dissolved in non-classical times, causing the cultural synthesis to fall apart. The classical repose is nothing but this firm synthesis of individual and community. When the self-conscious split sets in the cultural expressions must needs lack inner poise, forcing them to search for outward devices of security, a trend concomitant to all forms of alienation.

I

THE HISTORICAL CONCEPT OF ALIENATION

> America is said to be the arena on which the battle of
> freedom is to be fought; but surely it cannot be freedom
> in a merely political sense that is meant.
>
> Thoreau

1. AWARENESS, HUMAN AND HISTORICAL

To speak about alienation is to speak about ourselves. This is the problem. For although we know that 'ourselves' in the social framework is merely another copy of countless other selves, in our mind we fondle the uniqueness of our own self. That is our personal problem. It is also a community confusion. Separation is the fact, while conformity is the urgency. The self feels separated from the species, while the collective, in order to survive, demands the levelling of the self. The new technocratic order indeed solves the problem by levelling the self to satisfy the collective. At a price.

The confusion in the evaluation of our age can no better be indicated than by the confusion about the notion of alienation. It is caused, no doubt, by two factors. One lies in the multifarious aspects of the concept, the other in the highly emotional sub-contents which, every time it plays a part in our conversation or discourse, seem to boil to the surface and distort its reality. Each of us harbors a private brand of estrangement which is limited by either insufficient instruction in this matter, or by personal experiences.

As an example of the difficulties, which anyone determined to cut through this chaotic maze, will encounter, I should like to mention my experience with a friendly lady who once asked my opinion on this very subject. When I had started my exposition with careful hesitation, and arrived half-way in my second sentence, she interrupted me with the declaration that it was not true and she did not believe anything of it. Amazed by the impatience of this very amiable person whom I knew as intelligent and a professor of pediatrics at that, I saw no point in returning to my efforts and let her do her explaining, which brought out the revelation that to her alienation was simply equated with insanity. The fact that this lady, living in a medical world, knew the notion only in a specialized technical sense, makes the anecdote hardly worth relating, but the vehemence with which she defended her position does. It points to the problem of arriving at a poised and reasonable contemplation of one of the major phenomena of modern existence.

The confusion unfortunately is aggravated by those popular sociologists who, far from seeing social change in its historical continuity, treat social disturbances as isolated cases, preferably with broad accents of sentimentality. It is then that alienation comes to be undestood as a minority distress, of the negro, the Bowery bum, the homosexual, the criminal. Sometimes it becomes a minority's pride and honor. I know a student whose intelligence has greatly suffered from this kind of sentimental sociology, and being restive, frustrated and hopelessly stuck in his studies, prides himself on belonging to an élite of 'alienated intellectuals'. Once I made the thoughtless error of trying to enlighten him on the universal nature of his problem, and of explaining that the historical development of estrangement applies equally to every member of our society. He replied that he had an important date and had to leave in a rush. Which he did.

There are obviously various ways in which to deal with the occurrence of alienation, but whether viewed legally, medically, sociologically, psychologically, or historically, it remains a tendency whose effects must not be confused with its cause. The disappearance of birds and insect-life, the fading and falling of leaves, and the discoloring of the fields can be depicted individually by poets and painters in accurate as well as perceptive terms; for the UNDERSTANDING of autumnal changes, however, one has to probe into the underlying biological causes which typify the principle of the Fall season. Similarly, the various characteristic effects which occur persistently in twentieth-century society, political apathy, social isolation, anomia, loss of identity, violence, addiction, primitivism, cult of the savage, cult of the image, and innumerable others, can, and must be studied separately by the specialist, but this can be done with success only if they be seen as outward signals of an underlying principle.

It is here that historical perspective is able to produce tentative order. The advantage of the historical discipline is that it provides a dimension of depth, that is continuity, in addition to that of historical context.

History means many things to many people, which is a part of its attraction, but one not inconvenient way of formulating its objectives is to say that it continually relates individual occurrences with a general principle, change with pattern, uniqueness with necessity, and that it can put these relations in temporal perspective. If we therefore find ourselves entrapped in the complexity of a contemporary problem, the historical order may, to a certain extent at least, provide a helpful regulative dimension.

Before we attempt this, however, it is obligatory to posit the problem of alienation in its most simple and human form, that is as it is known to all, in order to derive from this certain basic attributes to serve us as further guidelines. The earliest experience for the normal individual occurs in the early teens when he enters the historic period of adolescence. Thoroughly profound and intricate works of psychology have probed this area, but one does not have to be a trained analyst to know the essential experiences involved from one's own memory. Any adult can from his own case-history recognize in the behavior of the adolescent the dark feelings of awakening. The world which he knew, in which he was the center, the world which was entirely identified by his own projections and dreams, now is pierced through and invaded from the outside. He learns to know 'the other'. Gradually it dawns on him that there exist other autonomous systems of thinking outside his own; his self-centered cosmology is shattered: other planetarian orders emerge over his horizon. Even within his own family structure he learns to distinguish that his brothers and sisters have a world of their own, that his parents live in a world of their own, and while at school he is taught the difference between the subjective and objective, in his consciousness the idea of selfhood comes to prevail, and with this the separation of the self and the immediate environment starts. His mind drifts away from the old family cohesion, producing the by-product of loneliness. Consequently he desires new allegiances: the club, the gang, the girl. Another by-product is evident in his rebelliousness. In his frustration he needs scapegoats. He blames family, school, church, society as a whole, for his uprooted and derooted existence.

Clearly a great number of further symptoms could be added to this picture, which everyone will admit leaves out an infinite variety of tones and shades. But this rather superficial sketch can be enlightening inasmuch as it represents the best recognizable features of the problem, common to all. It is this first image of estrangement which is the primer for adult life. Its imprint is so strongly stamped on the mind that it leaves its scar as a constant trauma. For while the shock of adolescence seems unique, it will soon turn out to be only the first of a shock-wave of separations inherent in life.

This crude structure of estrangement may thus set some basic rules for our investigation. These are, it must be remembered, in themselves not of a historical nature, but merely the main features of an illustration of a particular human experience. In the first place it describes a psychological development which though recognized as common to all human awareness, is experienced as unique and extremely personal. Still wrapped up in the cocoon of his dream world, the adolescent is unable to see that what to him constitutes the most private and most authentic, is in reality the most common experience of maturing life. This contradicting pattern is at the bottom of many forms of alienation. There is an element of illusion which ironically belies the prime intentions of the age: the urge to burst out and discover the outside phenomena. The pride in one's own uniqueness is counterweighed by the pride of growing up and fitting into a conforming universal mold.

When the adolescent's eyes open to the world of things, that is of opportunities, a natural experience of freedom begins. The width and breadth of freedom seem unlimited in view of the multiple goals and directions which the objective world suggests to him. Yet at no time do more limitations and inner brakes thwart his stirring vitality; and later he will with Wordsworth look back on his childhood as "glorious in the might of heaven-born freedom".[1] One realm of freedom opens up, while another seems to close. But the qualities of these freedoms are dissimilar. They sustain a relationship of mutual negation: the real dialectic basis for most forms of existential estrangement. The dialectic in this is also evident in the third characteristic, that of the need in the adolescent to belong to a secure unit, or group, which tendency however is curiously encouraged by the separation from the family group. The act of estrangement from the original stock brings his grafting onto a new extraneous system, the club, the gang, the fraternity. Connected with this is, in the fourth place, the factor of abnormalcy. The disaffiliated state of the teenager is not always, but frequently accentuated to a neurotic degree. A situation of crisis is created which contradicts the normalcy of the biological process of growth.

Another concomitant of this basic feeling of estrangement can be observed in the search for originality, which at times may strike the outsider as queer and whimsical, but which seems to satisfy an inner

[1] *Ode: Intimations of Immortality.*

need in the adolescent. Yet the proclivity occurs precisely at the time when that which is most original and authentic in him is abandoned for a new order outside his subjective world. Finally the early experience of estrangement, which we call adolescent restiveness, is generally accepted as characteristic of that age. Yet when we analyze the emotional contents, as we have done above, we find that it is only an incipient phase of a development of maturing, living and growing old. Through the stages of marrying, begetting children, giving children in marriage, there is an increasing realization that man's life, while acquiring more and more tangible assets is a continuous disassociation from the early ideals and visions. While the adolescent, however, lives through his estrangement, unconscious of its universal meaning, the alienation at a later age is consciously analyzed as such.

The notion of alienation, about which we today speak so confusedly, thus traces its importance primarily from a common existential situation. What makes us concerned about it now is the fact that it has in our time emerged as a HISTORICAL situation. How is this possible? And how must we understand this? How can we transfer a predominantly human and psychological experience to a historical awareness? Why should the awakennig to the fact of an individual's separation from his original ideal be applicable to the collective consciousness of an age?

The answer cannot possibly be given in a way satisfactory to the requirements of strict scholarship. A theory propounding that the various ages of individual man are concurrent with corresponding periods in history is attractive, but cannot be substantiated in a cogent manner, and historians therefore balk at the idea of typifying eras as if they were natural seasons. Nevertheles, whether academically justified or not, throughout the ages the idea has been put forward that the principle of biological rise and fall is equally relevant to mankind as a whole as it is to man. Some of the early fathers of the Church, especially Augustine, believe this to be so. Goethe in his morphological vision sees man as a microcosmos whose personal development is repeated in the historical phases of mankind's macrocosmos. Some historians rejecting the cyclical theory of rise and fall, are willing to treat specific periods according to 'human' behavior, and for instance accept Kant's suggestion that the period of the Enlightenment is historically man's coming of age.[2] When, however, it comes to pronouncements which

---

[2] Kant, "Beantwortung der Frage: Was ist Aufklärung?" in *Kleine Schriften* (Neuwied, 1793), 34-51. It is perhaps a minor point, but I cannot refrain from remarking that by Kant's own standards mankind's coming of age obviously occurs earlier. Should we not rather say that the motto *"Sapere aude!* Habe

98501

declare that modern man has reached old age, as Spengler and his followers assert, the willingness turns into rejection.

In this connection a few suggestions must be made. If clearly one cannot chop the continuity of history into regular seasons and ages, neither can one ignore the fact that any historical account must somehow deal with human life. Although there are of course specialists for whom the study of history has never advanced beyond the stage of sorting out archives and documents and putting their data in a certain order, the true historian tries to evoke the vibrations of life in the past. History thus, far from being a kind of necropsy, rests fundamentally on the same vital energy which is the concern of say, biology. Secondly, it has become natural to us to treat nations and other congeries *en masse* according to the behavior of individuals. We have accepted the idea of the GENERAL WILL, assuming that the very personal factor of will power is transferable to the masses. We recognize a collective consciousness which binds people of the same era together, and from Jung we have learned the extent and depth of the collective unconsciousness. Lamprecht divides cultural development into periods which correspond to psychological qualities such as individualistic, subjectivistic, nervous, etc.[3] There are evidently indications that what is experienced individually can under certain circumstances manifest itself in an entire nation or society.

To return to the phenomenon of alienation, that which we have described as an individual development of awareness, in the twentieth century emerges as a collective awareness. That both are of a historical order is already clear by the notion of development. We have noted that the most simple form of alienation is realized over a life-span in increasing grades of consciousness, a process which clearly seems to establish its historicity. The justification of an historical exposition of cultural estrangement lies in the fact that from the time when it was first described (by Schiller), and first mentioned as *Entäusserung* (by Fichte), the notion has gone through a process of change in importance and scope.

It is not necessary to restrict oneself to explicit statements on the

---

Muth dich deines eigenen Verstandes zu bedienen!" is already characteristic for the Renaissance man? If one wants morphology at all, the Renaissance seems to be the true claimant for the distinction of coming of age.

[3] K. Lamprecht, *Moderne Geschichtswissenschaft* (Freiburg i/B, 1905), 50-51, 62. Cf. also Kurt Breysig, *Naturgeschichte und Menschheitsgeschichte* (Breslau, 1933), which tries to see the unity of the history of the world and that of man, and Frobenius, *Paideuma* (München, 1921), 58, 59.

estranging tendencies during the last two centuries. There are many forms of behavior, scholarly preferences, artistic tastes which unwittingly point to this development and in their sometimes casual innocence may illustrate its aspects as strikingly as the most penetrating expository demonstration. One could, for instance, devote a monograph to the relationship between alienation and the Romanticist's archetype of the Wanderer as he appears in *Die Winterreise* or in *Childe Harold*. Equally indicative may well be the configuration of the self-exiled stranger who flees his native environment in order to search for truth elsewhere. He may be a Byron or a Shelley who denounces his society; he may be an Eichendorff yearning for the Silesian forests, or a Chamisso for his ancestral castle of Boncourt. He may also be a Kierkegaard on an island in Copenhagen, or for that matter a Thoreau in seclusion and an Emerson leaving the ministry.

A note of caution, however, seems not superfluous. Are such vague, or sometimes not so vague, feelings of self-estrangement, one may ask, not possible, and indeed not evident, at all times? They are, and it would be a light burden to supply some examples. In fact, we may as well realize from the onset that alienation has throughout the history of the Christian era been recognized as inherent in man. The fall of Adam signifies the separation of the body from the soul, a split which causes the continuous frustration of man on earth. It is reconciled only by the appearance of Christ, and the author of the Epistle to the Ephesians declares that since this event the believers are no more aliens to the eternal commonwealth.[4] In spite of this one cannot say that man on the whole during the classical periods of Christian culture demonstrates much of his frustration in the terrestrial order. This only becomes really apparent for the first time in the nineteenth century, but then in most cases without the Christian connotations. Whenever such feelings of social exile are expressed, the native paradise of bliss is not the new Jerusalem "prepared as a bride adorned for her husband",[5] or the heavenly city of Augustine, but rather an Arcadia of the past or a Utopia of the future. The awareness, first expressed by a few thinkers and poets in the early nineteenth century and growing to more and more general proportions in our time, is not a despair about a lost eternity. At least it is not realized as such. It is rather the recognition of an unbridgeable chasm between individual and species, man and society.

[4]   See III, 1, notes 16, 17, 18.
[5]   *Rev.* 21, 2.

Those cultural expressions which we can acknowledge as representing alienation are from the beginning vague and ambiguous, qualities which introduce the characteristic confusions of the problem. Hegel may be very specific and precise about it, but his formulation sets only the basic schematic pattern. With the advance of the nineteenth century, when more and more authors comment on it, more and more artists, poets and playwrights reflect it in their work, and the historical consciousness in general increases, Hegel's simple logical outlines of alienation appear as a multiple patchwork, a mosaic of fragments of alienation, most of which have abandoned the context of the whole composition.

2. ESTRANGEMENT, ITS VERSIONS AND VARIETIES

Before we try to restore the composition, it may serve our purpose if we take a look at the scattered individual pieces first, and from there proceed to understand the cultural composite. The least we are at this point able to acknowledge is that the sense of alienation is not frustration, distress, loneliness, rebelliousness, apathy in itself. Nor is it separation in itself. A divorcée is estranged from her husband, but not necessarily estranged in the particular social or cultural sense. An immigrant of peasant stock, transplanted to the American metropolitan bustle must feel utterly foreign at times, and probably often isolated and lonely; yet this experience in itself does not constitute the phenomenon with which we are dealing here. Nor do Negroes discriminated against, homosexuals isolated, or beatniks dislocated, represent alienation by their sheer minority plight. Since on the basis of the prototypes which we presented above, estrangement is a concurrent product of growing, maturing, aging, it must, in order to be culturally understood, be predicated on a sense of historical inevitability and inexorable destiny. When this underlying principle is not recognized, the presentation of the various forms of alienation merely results in a description of outward signs, telling effects, which misses the point of the inward motivation and direction.

Although these forms naturally differ greatly, it does not mean that they have no aspect in common. Essentially they all are varieties of SEPARATION. They represent the tendency of bifurcation, often intensified to the degree of diffusion, or an irreparable split. Separation may be felt after the crisis year of 410 A.D. when Augustine differentiates two cities, or in our scientific times when we speak about the two

Cultures. But it may also be in the order of 'lonely crowds' and 'disinherited minds'. The adolescent separated from the stem to which he belongs is our prototype here with his accompanying dismay about the experience of an unreasonable paradox. In a vision about his deceased father a Dutch poet wonders:

> How is it then that this man
> of my own identical stock
> must find this fearful end? [6]

as if awaking to the recognition that his father's experience (dying) is outside his own realm. The separation from his 'own identical stock' is now transferred to society in general and turns into a basic principle:

> One day one helps the other,
> but in this life not yet;
> we are strangers for each other,
> forgive it, but don't forget.

Separation thus here does not mean the act of severance, but rather the awakening to the fact of man's fundamental state of severance. It is not the disjunction of two spheres previously united, but the realization that the old unity was an illusion. That one needs two eyes to see reality's perspective.

Sometimes the distinction is made between alienation and SELF-ALIENATION, causing a confusion, which however is of a minor nature. Originally the term alienation is a legal designation, applying to the transfer of the ownership of goods. As such it occurs in the work of Grotius, who uses the Latin verb *alieno*. If, however, the subjective self, or rather a part of its consciousness is exported so to speak to the outside world and incorporated in the phenomena, the self may be said to be estranged, for it seems to behave like an object, and indeed becomes object. Needless to say that this distinction of self-alienation is not extraordinarily useful. For the problem as it is analyzed here and as it takes its place in contemporary discussion is usually about the objectivation of the self, and the word self-alienation has become rather meaningless, except as a stylistic variation. A French author, noting that some forms of alienation are dialectic and others not, indicates

[6]   J. W. F. Weremeus Buning, "In Memoriam Patris", *Verzamelde Verzen* (Amsterdam, 1941), 68.

the latter by the word *extranéation*,[7] meaning an exteriorization of the self which is not dialectically to return back into the consciousness, in other words probably an estrangement not realized by the subject itself. If a man is made into a cog of the organization machine, his identity can be said to be lost in the mechanistic routine, extraneated in the objects of his work. He can be quite satified with his situation and thus not be aware of the estrangement. If he on the other hand realizes it and suffers from the thought, the extraneation would according to this theory dialectically become alienation. Such distinctions again lose their meaning in practice, since the moments of consciousness and self-consciousness are so personal and hidden for the outsider, that the terms of the dialectic make merely a play of words. Traditionally, alienation, self-alienation, extraneation, as well as the German expressions *Entäusserung* and *Entfremdung* are constantly interchanged.

When the substance of the I imparts itself to the phenomenal world of the non-I, in Fichte's terms, the former actually becomes 'thing'. This process of OBJECTIVATION represents the true core of all estrangement. A transformation of quality takes place, a part of the subject in the act of communication becomes objective. In language, for instance, the speaker's individual thought content is by means of the voice conveyed to the 'other', and the thought becomes public domain. It is in the problem of objectivation that the real differences in the assessment of the extent and quality of estrangement starts. It can on the one hand be argued that from the moment the subjectivity imparts itself to the world of objects, the self is already alienated. On the other hand, Marx who sees alienation not as an inherent human factor, but exclusively as one of the plagues of the bourgeois régime, is against the identification of objectivation and alienation. Only one particular brand of objectivation is rejected, namely when it is 'the dehumanization (*Entwirklichung*) of the worker'.[8] At the appropriate place this will be elaborated further. Here it should be noted from the outset that an investigation of the TOTAL aspect of alienation in the cultural sense must necessarily be encyclopedic in its scope, and inevitably accept all human objectivation as fundamental estrangement. Alienation on this basis is not an evil brought on mankind by a specific group, but a natural development. No scapegoats then are to be sent into the desert, no Fascists, Jews, Marxists, Capitalists, Jesuits, Freemasons, Christians, or Atheists to be blamed for the process of dehumanization which marks the contem-

---

7   Pierre Naville, *De l'aliénation à la jouissance* (Paris, 1957), 55-56.
8   Marx, Zur Kritik der Nationalökonomie, *Frühe Schriften*, I, 561.

porary physiognomy. If one recognizes the importance of learning the principle rather than a few selected varieties of alienation, objectivation is one of the significant keys to the understanding of the cultural universality of estrangement.

All objectivation, as we have indicated here, is EXTERIORIZATION inasmuch as the substance of the self is as it were turned inside out, and something which originally exists on the strength of its inward privacy adopts an exterior form in which it is publicized. No one can miss the importance of this in an age of advertisement, and exteriorization takes on a specific function with the appearance of today's guiding standard: the Image.[9] In the image the exterior stamp comes to be accepted as the essence which it originally only represents. When in our existence the brilliant wrappings of the products are the primary interest of seller and consumer with a proportionate deterioration of the substance which the wrapping contains, we are obviously victims of exteriorization. When poetry becomes a display of disconnected striking metaphors, whatever its thrill, the poetic conveyance rests exclusively on its outward manifestations. Exteriorization plays an important role in social communications when the mere existence of legislation appears as valid without the necessary edorsement of the spirit of law which prompts legal action in the first place. It is becoming common around the world, but in this country it has been a national attitude from the beginning. "If the American displayed a cavalier disrespect for law and an abiding suspicion of lawyers, he venerated Law."[10] What shows up here is a belief in the formula, not only and not primarily in the scientific meaning, but as a magic expression which takes care of man's troubles by the mere act of being promulgated. It signifies the confidence in the justification of mechanical arrangements which, abandoning their quality of tool, have acquired the status of achievement.

Thus the process of exteriorization leads easily to a confusion of ends and means. In a sense these terms indicate a relation between interior and exterior qualities, but also, and more importantly, a difference in autonomous and functional value. All tools and machines "have a tendency to become independent of their creator and to appear as

---

[9]   Among the works devoted to this phenomenon: Kenneth Boulding, *The Image* (Ann Arbor, 1956), and Daniel J. Boorstin, *The Image* (New York, 1962), as well as *America and the Image of Europe* (New York, 1960). Also Charles Y. Glock, "Images of Man and Public Opinion", *The Public Opinion Quarterly*, XXVIII, 4 (1964), 539-547.
[10]   H. S. Commager, *The American Mind* (New Haven, 1950), 19.

foreign to him".[11] This not only holds true in technology, but even more so in artistic fields. If for instance, the instrumentality of the image is converted into a desirable goal, and poetic imagery becomes an autonomous asset, the essence of poetry is highly limited in its expression. Here the means have usurped the place of the end. But the reverse can be observed too. If what we presume is true, and many Sunday worshippers use their affiliation with a specific church as a status emblem or as a club service, the original value of religion clearly has become a function in the socal framework and the end has been transformed into an instrument. Ends and means in modern art and letters are persistently confused, and so they are in the world of commerce where the quality of the advertised image is often more important than the quality of the commodity. They are confused in the world of journalism where the 'story' of the news becomes essential instead of the event itself. They are no less mixed up in the academic administration when more usually than not credits, points and grades are the first objectives and the substance of learning is only so many stepping stones towards a degree. While scholarly works are originally supposed to be statements of knowledge and discovery, they have nowadays too often turned into mere requirements for tenure and promotion. To what extent the exchange of ends and means is connected with the building up of an image, may be illustrated by an evaluation of the Kennedy administration in the *New York Times*.[12] In a leading article the readers are told that the president's main achievement was the gathering around the White House of young scholarly intellectuals to advise him. This is no sarcasm. On the contrary, the serious tone of the article merely demonstrates how also in politics and government ways and means are mistaken for achievement.

Sometimes the tendency of alienation is rooted in the insistence on mistaking part for the whole. This *pars-pro-toto* treatment derives frequently from the element of distress and frustration accompanying the act of separation which marks all estrangement. A part is severed from the whole and comes to be isolated and accepted as a new autonomous whole. The elderly man who views the new sprouting family life of his married children from a distance, who has retired from his job into an isolated existence, lives, though he be very much alive and healthy, in a world separated from the main circulation of life. There are also

---

[11] F. Heinemann, *Existentialism and the Modern Predicament* (New York, 1958), 17.
[12] *New York Times* (December 2, 1963).

social ghettos where a new autonomy has superseded the universal laws of living-together, whether this is in Harlem, the Bowery, Levittown or Park Avenue. Similarly there are mental enclaves where the parochial ideology is imposed on the variety and fullness of organic life. There are Marxists who must submit all the expressions of cultural vitality to their social and political determinism, and there are psychiatrists forever engaged in the symptomatic attempt to bring every single human move under the doctrine of libido. The academic world is pre-eminently suitable for the *pars-pro-toto* trend, for specialization and parochialism are agreeable neighbors. We are not thinking in terms of fanaticism here. Our age is possibly less fanatical than previous ones. Nor can it be said that parochialism is a novelty. We are simply concerned with the question as to what extent specific individual proclivities in our time have become, or tend to become, collective trends which permeate all the levels and fields of society. On the *pars-pro-toto* basis painters and sculptors may develop one particular side of the classical technique in their profession. In drama, which is by its very nature the most composite mode of literature, one can in the twentieth century observe new manners of technique abandoning the fullness of the traditional drama. The universality of the Greek tragedy is only inadequately expressed in Aristotle's formula of the six components plot, character, style, thought content, scenic form, song.[13] It represents an integral synthesis of all the arts. In much of the modern drama, however, one of the basic ingredients, say spectacularity or character development, is frequently elaborated almost exclusively, and at the expense of the total integration.

On the sociological scene alienation often occurs as ROOTLESSNESS in the sense of the restless and restive nature which characterizes the modern temper. While this is becoming more and more evident in European countries, mobility has been one of the oldest and most conspicuous traits of American life.[14] The traditional roots of man lie naturally and almost unconsciously in his loyalties to the native soil, church, and community, which are never questioned or challenged from the outside. These loyalties make him an inseparable part of his immediate setting and he is thus organically embedded in indigenous security. Most of our loyalties in contrast, are acquired, seem deliberate and usually of a partisan nature. They may be given to the Yankees or the Dodgers, but are without a real experience of identity. In this world

[13]   Aristotle, *Poet.*, VI, 9.
[14]   George W. Pierson, "A restless Temper ...", *American Historical Review*, LXIX, 4 (1964).

we change our tastes and preferences as easily as our linen, and it is understandable that under such circumstances a deep-rooted security is all but absent. Consequently this tendency is also reflected in the uncertain eclesticism of artistic, architectural or literary style, which, with the classical tradition broken up, must frequently seek refuge in technical inventions and imitations of unrelated cultures. Sociologists have found a special area of rootlessness in the disturbances called *anomia*. The word, in Greek meaning without law, has in the modern context nothing to do with lawlessness, but rather with a state of disorganization where all norms and directions are missing. Unfortunately those ignorant about the background and scope of alienation, of which anomia is only a small aspect, often confuse the two terms. It not infrequently represents a case of the "modishness in which sophisticated words like *alienation, anomia, massification* are used freely but with little attention to what these complicated words represent".[15] Anomia is that kind of alienation which man experiences in the mass-absorption of the modern industrial system, when his self is incorporated as just another 'thing' in the mechanism of the production apparatus. It is sometimes connected with political apathy, or more negatively, with cynicism towards the efficacy and justice of democratic procedures. Political alienation then can be said to be a reflection of anomia, as a feeling of being threatened and controlled by outside forces.[16]

In the familiar picture of the worker, entering the factory to place himself at the assembly line as a part of the machine, we can without strain recognize the principle of DEHUMANIZATION. Thus it is easily linked up with the notion of anomia. But whereas anomia usually implies an element of suffering, it would be totally incorrect to assume that all alienation is experienced as a tragic burden. On the contrary, it often manifests itself in blithe confidence. The reason why Lyndon Johnson is so fond of telling us that it is not the man but the system that counts in our society, is that he knows it will strike a popular note. Contemporary man has quietly accepted that there is nothing wrong with the 'system', and if there are abuses and derailments still, he assumes that these can be put right by even better and more adjustments of man to the system.

This encouraged erosion of human responsibilities is one of the most

---

[15] Daniel Bell, "The Sociology of Work", *New York Review of Books* (October 22, 1964).
[16] E. L. McDill and J. C. Ridley, "Status, Anomia, Political alienation, and Political participation", *American Journal of Sociology*, LXVIII, 2 (1962).

serious implications of alienation, and one far more detrimental to the unfolding of our social potential than the 'suffering' kinds selected by the popular treatments of this subject. It is a hidden blight cloaked in an illusion of happiness. The modern social bliss as a state of absolute adjustment dehumanizes man's intelligence by reducing it to a link in the machine. When social Darwinism with its idea of the ruthless 'fittest' had become untenable, the doctrine of the mindless 'fitter-in' was a convenient successor. On its historical consequences one cannot speculate here. But as a form of estrangement from an original human dignity, happiness in dehumanization is one of the most ominous facts of the twentieth century.

Not surprisingly, it finds its natural reflection in the arts and literature of our time. The Futurists on the whole have unbridled confidence in the future of the machine, and their paintings show the grind and the crush of technology with defiant *élan*. The new architecture of the metropolitan society erects structures which, whatever one's judgment on their esthetic aspirations, have grown beyond the human scale. Masereel's woodcuts show them in stark black and white contraptions which, like the machine settings of Meyerhold and Tairov, allow some human flesh to be incorporated in the entanglement.

The dehumanization of man's existence can also be stressed by that form of alienation which appears as cultural ABSTRACTION. Man grown old, isolated from the vital mainstream of society, starts to analyze emotions, events, and experiences which previously were merely part of his actions. The act of love itself becomes for him a theoretical reflection, which at best can produce wisdom, but in itself is only a substitute for the real thing. This is simply an illustration of the analytic disposition which emerges in a state of estrangement, and which typifies our age. Whether this is caused by the predominance of scientific thinking, can be left aside. At any rate our conception of science itself has changed from an explanation of tangible phenomena in man's daily life to a body of abstract knowledge, far beyond the reach of all but a few specialists. It is hard to determine whether in this case one must see nature as alienated from man, or vice versa, man as having stepped out of nature. Now also the image which man has of his natural self becomes abstracted. One can see abstraction entering into the late nineteenth-century drama with Wedekind's and later Strindberg's characters, which set the pattern for the Expressionist playwrights, including Brecht. One sees it in Tschelitchew's geometrical derivations from the human body, and in the development of abstract art through all the successive stages until Mondrian, seeking the purest expression of being, ends up with a structure of squares as the schematic formula of life. Vitality which previously was mere experience, elusive to the analytic brain, now is isolated and subjected to scholarly disciplines. Since universities have claimed the very unscientific expressions of poetry, politics or news reporting as their material, there is nothing left which cannot in this age of analysis be put into abstractions.

This schematic survey is not supposed to be more than a preliminary reconnaissance around the spreading complexities of the principle of alienation. The list is by no means exhaustive. Nor are the variations mutually exclusive, for it will be seen that in actuality they must frequently overlap. But if one tolerates the shortcomings inherent in theoretical breakdowns, this introductory presentation can serve, I hope, as a primer to the understanding of the breadth and depth of our problem.

From this vantage-point we can at least be clear about a few basic elements which provide us with a firm footing. In the first place, the preceding analysis makes it clear that alienation is not a particular distress of a particular minority group, but a development, historically proceeding and universally felt. It is not something imposed upon man by outside forces, but a realization in man's own mind. Naturally, he may experience the rat-race of modern competitive life, the hostility of metropolitan existence, the conformity of managerial organization as powers threatening his authentic individuality. But feelings of misery under the pressure of overwhelming energies from outside are a continuous experience in mankind and as old as its history. That which in human suffering in general, however, comes to be realized as estrangement is an awareness that man is drifting away from his original goals. He is uprooted, exteriorized, objectified, abstracted, so to speak, from his origin.

It cannot be stressed enough that this awareness is of a universal nature; in other words it is a historical, not a personal or group phenomenon, and one which does not allow anyone to escape its impact. It is therefore useless to assume a self-righteous attitude and look around for scapegoats. This is natural enough, and it belongs itself in the climate of alienation, witness the adolescent blaming the previous generation for the shortcomings of society. It is a natural attitude in general of blaming the 'world', that vague monstrosity, for one's separateness. But it is not the Industrial Revolution which is to blame, nor the Romantic movement, nor Capitalism, nor Nationalism, nor any other predominant social force of the nineteenth century. These and similar factors merely act as catalysts in the process of intensified awareness. Disturbances of alienation are not caused by traps and snares of human exploitation, nor by the ruthless selfishness of social Darwinism, nor by a political system of fascist, communist or democratic persuasion. Economic exploitation and political corruption of one kind or other have never ceased to exert their pressures in history. But cultural alienation is a new motif in Western civilization, growing more and more firmly established in the consciousness of man during the previous century and becoming a haunting theme in the minds of our age. It is thus related to the increased historical consciousness developing in the same period, and similarly concurrent with the changes in the understanding and meaning of the notion of culture.

If estrangement is not primarily about social discontent, loneliness, minority distress, cultural frustration, what is the underlying stirring factor causing all these to appear like warts and boils on a skin? When we remarked that there exists a curious discrepancy between the incertitude of the contemporary outlook and the possession of our newly-won liberties, a situation was implied which one could call (for lack of a better term) a dialectical crisis, whereby two historical forces mutually negate and sustain each other. The one is of a liberating energy, the other of a destructive authority. The adolescent finding the world opening to him, sees his freedom negated by a frustrating and self-conscious confusion. The retired old man, once released from the tension of the organization machine, sees his freedom negated by a nostalgia for the past where he used to suffer.

There is obviously no room here for an elaborate logical or psychological probing of the mechanics of alienation. All important is the understanding that its natural feeling of tension is produced and sustained by the effect of two countermotions: opportunity and frustration. Cultural neurosis, which is manifest in all the intellectual and artistic achievements of the age, is caused simply by the gap between opportunity and its satisfaction. It is most patently present in the American society where opportunities in general have been more abundant than anywhere else in the course of history, and where the lack of cultural fulfilment is most painfully felt. While man has never before been so well equipped with tools and knowledge to help himself, he has rarely found himself less satisfied and at rest in his own world. The recently discovered tribe of the Bindibu in central Australia, living in one of the most inhospitable areas of the world, has in its stone-age existence a range of opportunity that must seem nil compared by our standards. Yet they are a perfectly happy, friendly and poised breed of people who know no disputes, politics, leaders, organization or war.

Cultural estrangement thus is not a fact or an event, but a ratio of freedom, determined by the magnitudes of opportunity and fulfilment. Since in human society these two factors become concrete in the mutual entanglement of work and play elements, our specific investigation must needs start from here. Work and play both become important entities in nineteenth-century thinking, as part of the increasing historical and cultural consciousness, and both clearly relate to the idea of freedom. Therefore, before we enter into the aspects of the alienation of play and work, we ought to make it plain to ourselves that at the root of all alienation there lies the unrest of freedom which, complex and inscrutable as it appears, must yet be accounted for within the cultural scope of our theme.

3. FREEDOM, ITS OPPORTUNITY AND UNFULFILLMENT

It will be agreed that nothing is more hazardous than venturing into the emotional climate of freedom, and nothing more inviting to blunt generalizations which are unsuitable for historical narration and penetration. The notion of liberty is intimately linked to man's ideal state of happiness, whatever it be, which itself is such an elusive proposition that any sensible discourse on it is bound to fail in the perplexity of emotional content. In our particular pursuit we cannot, and should not, attempt much more than outlining the problem, and placing it historically in the perspective of estrangement. We will be excused, I trust, from either producing a metaphysical structure, or a panoramic view of the pragmatic uses of freedom, and satisfy ourselves with a few fundamental suggestions on which all can agree.

It is significant that the man who first probed into the complex of alienation, spent his entire life championing the cause of liberty and exploring the ways to establish a state of freedom in man's mind. From *Die Räuber* (1781) to *Wilhelm Tell* (1804) Schiller's plays, poems and essays emerge within 'the scheme of freedom', in Goethe's words. Schiller follows the early events of the French Revolution with approval, and he himself is, through the revolutionary spirit of his plays, popular with the Jacobins. But the historical developments after 1792 and the ensuing Terror raise doubts in his mind about the future of political liberties, if they are not brought into harmony with a controlling principle. About the nature of this principle he is unsure at first. With foresight he predicts that only a dictatorship can come from an un- checked yielding to the masses, and he withdraws in disgust from any political action. Instead he begins his search for the essentials of freedom. The historic result appears in his *Letters on the Esthetic Education* (1795) in which he develops a theory of freedom, partly Kantian, partly highly original, leading to the Utopia of an Esthetic State. The letters constitute the earliest primer of alienation, a concept never named so by Schiller, but clearly described by him in his analysis of the contemporary situation. This degrading condition, according to Schiller, can only be overcome if mankind is educated for the Esthetic State, whose constitution is "to give freedom through freedom". It is the third and highest state in the development of mankind, appearing after the dynamic realm, where weapons and power decide, and the ethical state of duties, where 'the majesty of law' rules by curtailing man's will. The Esthetic State however is the 'joyful realm of play', in which man's esthetic dignity "removes all the chains of relationships from man, and frees him from all physical and moral coercion".[17]

The Esthetic State is an abstraction, in no way related to the practi- cal and political exigencies from which governments and constitutions arise. Schiller himself does not believe that his Utopia can exist other than in any 'harmonious soul'.[18] It is, however, not his rather escapist idealism which is under scrutiny here, but the structure of freedom it- self. This, in Schiller's conception, is a harmonious balance, an absolute freedom, embracing and uniting the particular freedoms which man's pluralistic mind projects *vis-à-vis* individual everyday problems. They can be classed as belonging on the one hand to the sensate, and on the

---

[17] Schiller, *Werke (Horenausgabe)*, XI, 113. It is one of the remarkable aspects of Schiller's theory that it defines freedom positively, in contrast to most concep- tions. Hobbes for instances suggests (*Leviathan*, Cambridge, 1904, 147) that "Lib- erty, or Freedome, signifieth (properly) the absence of opposition." See also Oscar and Mary Handlin, *The Dimensions of Liberty* (Cambridge, Mass., 1961), 10, and Mortimer Adler, *The Idea of Freedom* (Garden City, 1958), 112.
[18] Schiller, *ibid.*, XI, 116. Schiller, through Goethe and W. von Humboldt, was greatly influenced by the Greek idea of harmony. Although there are no indica- tions that Schiller knew Plato's *Republic*, there are striking similarities between this work and the *Letters*. As to Schiller's final remark, it compares with the end of the *Republic*, when to Glaucon's doubting question where such a state could exist, Plato answers that it can only be understood as a "pattern laid up in heaven" (IX, 592).

other to the intelligent urges which react to each other in a sort of dialectical tension. For practical purposes one could say that these two polar concepts relate as political and moral freedom.

It is evident that this manner of reasoning is rather abstract, not to say naive to our pragmatic mind. It suggests an intellectual evading of life which Schiller elsewhere urges in verse:

> Flee then from the confines of the senses
> Into liberty of thought,
> And the ghost of fear will disappear.[19]

But whatever may or may not be of lasting validity in his conception of absolute freedom, at this point it is important for us to observe that, although he gets lost in theoretical speculations, he at least dares to ask the essential questions. As so often scholarship is better served by profound confusion than by puny truths, so Schiller's deficient treatment marks a historic moment. Even if one cannot demonstrate what exactly is the extent of Schiller's influence on Hegel's concept of history and liberty, or on the Communist Manifesto [20] there is no denying that the *Esthetic Letters* open up a new era of historical consciousness. In a sense this represents a consciousness of the age, reflected in a stream of *Zeitkritiken*; in another sense one can call it a self-consciousness reflected in the study of alienation, for instance. But above all, it is a consciousness of freedom. The chief question as put forward by Schiller, reduced to its most simple schematic form, is how can man with the advancement of political liberties retain the dignity of moral freedom? In other words, how can the expansion of individual rights on an egalitarian basis take place without ending up in a despotism of the masses? It is an old problem, which indeed appears as one of the major themes in Plato's Republic. In the nineteenth century, however, the growing separation of political and moral freedom produces an entirely new content of awareness: the ultimate content of all alienation.

How must we understand this concretely? Probably the most meaningful way to present the estrangement in the consciousness of freedom is to relate it to the contemporary widening of the cleft between man

[19]   "Das Ideal und das Leben", *Ibid.*, XVII, 141.
[20]   Heinrich Popitz, in *Der entfremdete Mensch* (Basel, 1953), 28, thinks that the ultimate consequences of Schiller's *Letters* are realized in the Communist Manifesto.

and society, person and group, individual and collective. In these rather conventional, but fundamental contrasts the dialectic of moral and political liberties finds its expression, and they will, among other factors, guide us through subsequent chapters. Schiller himself stresses the separation of individual and society in his sixth letter where he complains that all the advantages of the age go to the species and the disadvantages to the individual. The lack of harmony which he sees in his time, becomes aggravated during the next century, until in the figures of Kierkegaard and Marx the ideas of individual and collective freedom are entirely set apart from each other, each finding its own promoter.

Hegel, somewhat earlier, presents the history of the world as a growing awareness of freedom, not indeed, as a story of liberty, as Croce inaccurately thinks, but as "the progress in the consciousness of freedom, a progress which we must fathom in its necessity".[21] Whereas in the Orient only one, the despot, is known as free, with the Greeks a few are free; it is only in modern times that man as such is recognized as free. Croce, like most nineteenth-century thinkers highly dependent on Hegel but struggling for his own identity, changes Hegel's formula by viewing history as eternally created by liberty.[22] Marx, in contrast, sees very little freedom already established. Hegel's notion that all men are free is denied by the facts. The workers are still the slaves of the capitalistic production machine, and only when the proletariat seizes power and a classless society is founded can freedom become realized. The freedom of the Communist Manifesto postulates concrete achievements such as the abolition of private property, the centralization of credit in a state bank, centralization of the means of transport and communications in the hand of the state. While for Hegel history is a progressive realization of liberty, for Marx it is the way to socialization. Without such socialization Hegel's conception of freedom seems to Marx only a fetish, that is an empty right which cannot be exercised.[23] Whereas Marx is planning the revolution to establish a collective freedom, Kierkegaard in the same period revolts against the massification of society. The levelling process which is curtailing the freedom of the individual means to him an attack on freedom itself, as it can only be realized individually. In contrast to Croce's thinking, Kierkegaard

---

[21]   Hegel, *Phil. d. Geschichte*, Einl., II, a.
[22]   B. Croce, *History as the Story of Liberty* (New York, 1941), 59.
[23]   Sidney Hook, *From Hegel to Marx* (Ann Arbor, 1962), 40.

understands the historical process as a 'determination of necessity' in
which there is no more freedom than in nature. Only the individual's
absolute choice of Either-or is free. [24] The organization of the masses
thus has a corrupting influence on the real spiritual emancipation of
man.

These conflicting conceptions of freedom are part of a century which
is, among other things, one of emancipation. This applies to social
minority groups, as well as to whole nations separating themselves from
centuries old empires. In this climate of liberty-conscious thinking a
great number of confusing theories on freedom are being launched
which it is not our task to arrange in a neat classification. It merely
suffices here to see that they all relate to a dialectic polarity of freedom
which expresses itself socially in the antithesis of individual and society.
It is not a matter for philosophers and sociologists only. The theme
reverberates as insistently in the works of literary figures.

Ricarda Huch, who is not only one of Germany's best female poets,
but also a perceptive essayist, devotes a study to the de-personalization
of man, which she bases on the incapability of modern man to be at the
same time an individual and communal person.[25] Matthew Arnold, who
wrestles with the problem of how to expand culture without falling
into anarchy, warns that the worship of human freedom as an end is as
disastrous as worshipping machines as an end, and he contrasts the
freedom of doing what one likes to that of following one's reason in
order to attain perfection.[26] In the United States the idea of liberty to
the Transcendentalists revolves around the same dialectic as is evident
in continental thinking. Emerson, during most of his life, tries to reconcile the benefits of solitude with integration in society. And Thoreau,
observing the imbalance of the national goals of his age, cries out:
"What is the value of any political freedom, but as a means to moral
freedom?" [27] The latter he finds lacking.

If we cannot presume to have settled all the problems raised by the
notion of freedom, we may at least hope to have demonstrated that
freedom does not simply deal with the acquisition and defense of an
infinite number of RIGHTS, but with a dialectical situation in which
JUSTICE towards individual as well as collective stands in a constantly
critical tension. Any loss or failing of this relationship which is not of

24 Kierkegaard, *Either-Or*, V.
25 Ricarda Huch, *Entpersönlichung* (Leipzig, 1922), 12.
26 M. Arnold, *Culture and Anarchy* (New York, 1925), 71.
27 Thoreau, *Writings* (Boston, 1906), Riverside Ed., IV, 477.

an intellectual order, but totally human and vital, produces an unrest in society, shattering the creative harmony of its cultural manifestations. In this enquiry the notion of freedom will not be mentioned frequently, since it would only encourage confusions. Yet it will always be behind the question of estrangement as the existential content of modern man's split-consciousness.

If, one analyses the place of the artist in contemporary culture in terms of alienation, the examination can be focused on the discrepancy between his freedom as an authentic painter and the opportunities offered to him by an organized modern society. In this connection the question may arise whether the freedom of the artist who spends his life searching for the objectivation of an inner vision without being able to sell a single picture (van Gogh), is not infinitely more normal than the freedom of one who directs a particular technique to a particular dealer's market and is successfully fashionable in the museums of modern art. It is obvious that the two cases do not exclude each other, but they do point to different motivations. In the first one can easily recognize a factor of moral liberty, as contrasted, in the second instance, to that of a far greater freedom of opportunities. Similarly, the playwright who is forever concerned about responding to the demands of modern professional show-bussines, as it is rightly called, must needs be a specialist whose technique is concentrated on a few particular forms that work. It would be naive and historically incorrect to believe that the drama forms of previous periods were not subjected to professional and popular pressures. They were. Yet the results show that they were written in a comprehensive technique, in which an Aeschylus, a Marlowe, a Lope de Vega, a Corneille, a Schiller integrate vision, poetic expression, unity of thought, psychological analysis and scenic effect. Their almost unrestricted freedom of vision contrasts with the narrow poetic scope of the modern playwright, who, no doubt, has an incomparably larger audience available.

Education, as we all know, has traditionally been linked with the awareness of cultural freedom, and its promotion offered as a necessity for social emancipations of many kinds. Rightly so. The gathering of ascertainable facts and the establishing of their mutual relationships contributes to the eradication of constricting prejudices, fears, and repressions. The democratic spirit as we have cultivated it is in a great measure the product of a wider and more intensive schooling. Education as it is originally conceived simply aims at the cultivation of intelligence, and its freedom lies foremost in self-discipline to be won through intellectual discipline. Twentieth-century education, under the stress of technocratic predominance, must in the first place produce specialists, and thus it serves the 'opportunities' far better than the older system, which aims primarily at the maturing of the mind.

What emerges here is a division between a freedom of inner conviction and that of opportunity, or a freedom to be and a freedom to have. They are normally very much intermingled in daily life. But today we may wonder whether the latter has not taken up our full attention, at the expense of the former. Viewed in the most schematic manner, freedom to be relates chiefly to quality, the other to quantity. Thus in our pluralistic outlook we collect not only things but also freedoms, as if they were the ordinary chattels and goods that belong to gracious living. It does not necessarily mean that we have somehow selected the wrong kind of freedom, but merely that we are not able to integrate the freedom of being with that of having.

This deficiency, if deficiency it be, shows up most conspicuously in our political attitudes and agitations. Not surprisingly, for the democratic dispensation under which we are at least nominally living, derives its meaning and existence from a basic awareness of liberty. Whether or not it is the best, as we think, or the least viable form of government as Plato tells us, or not a beneficial order at all, as Aristotle believes, depends on our conception of human freedom. If democracy aims at the fulfillment of the largest number of opportunities and appetites, we must be well on the way to historic greatness. If on the other hand Plato's and Aristotle's classical notion of freedom is correct, and freedom is primarily based on a harmony of the mind, then our democratic system is preparing us gradually for the machinery of despotism. Our pursuit here does not include the answer to this question; it simply tries to probe into the reasons why such alternatives exist in our mind.

Alienation is the predicament of unresolved alternatives. When Hegel closes the books on the classical Western culture, and as the last of the classics tries to encompass the whole in a system of reconciliation, he lays unwittingly the foundation for a new era. For instead of only being the last, he is also at the beginning of a new world in which the reconciling synthesis is lost, and man's consciousness split by unresolved alternatives. We do not have to remind ourselves all the time that in our daily relationships the choices are rarely black or white, doom or triumph, evil or beatitude. It is the reflecting mind which forces the entire complex of contemporary thrusts into dialectic alternatives. Whether this tendency is correct or false, helpful or harmful, is irrelevant. In this context it is first of all mandatory to study the phenomenon, to ask why it exists, and to know its extent.

Quantity against quality, opportunity against disposition, having against being – in these polarities our consciousness trembles. We handle our feelings by remote control. We need gadgets to experience life. In the fashionable confusion about alienation, we seem estranged from alienation. What are we alienated from, if not from essentials? The essential, the ground of birth and existence, lies abandoned behind us. In the Futurist's exaltation we have made a flying machine of our heart to speed to the peripheries of life and chant with Marinetti:

> Propeller! fierce propeller of my monoplane heart,
> free and formidable drill of rapture,
> do you not feel the dreadful obscurity crack
> under your piercing thrust? [28]

It is an inevitable flight, and there is no return. Velocity itself is our destination. Some will dream of the next planet. Others, the parachute in their hand, are preparing for the jump. These are the alternatives of our freedom.

[28]   F. T. Marinetti, *Le monoplan du pape* (Paris, 1912), 21:
Hélice! forte hélice de mon cœur monoplan,
formidable vrille enthousiaste et volontaire,
ne sens tu pas craquer les ténèbres exécrables
sous ton effort perçant?

II

LABOR, PLAY, CULTURE

> Culture has become objective and set itself up in op-
> position to the subjectivity which has engendered it.
> Ortega y Gasset

Culture thus understood as a product of human societies requires the analysis of those forces which produce it. That is, we must consider the constituent FACTORS which make culture. The word factor derives from the Latin *facio*, to make, and *factum* is the achievement of making If we ask ourselves which activity makes the cultural product, the concept of labor of course constitutes the easiest answer. Human work, however, in itself is obviously not enough to produce cultural achievements. Every one is involved in daily labor, but most of us can have little illusion that this immediately contributes to culture. All human societies know toil as the basic condition for existence, but not all of these are able to translate work into culture, and even those which do, go through many centuries of unrecorded history. Clearly the factor of labor needs the assistance of another agent to produce fruition.

A number of scholars, Burckhardt, Frobenius and Huizinga among them, have stressed the importance of the element of play for great cultural achievements. They have generally considered it disconnected from labor – legitimately so. But play in itself, cannot any more than labor, engender the social product which we call culture. When we therefore probe into the nature of modern Western civilization, an analysis of both play and labor in their reciprocal relationship will be needed to understand the structure of historical culture.

The nineteenth century is the age of labor. From the time that Adam Smith, in 1776, points out that man's labor is the real measure of the exchangeable value of commodities, daily work becomes a philosophical category on which reflective minds start to speculate. Our century is the age of tools, Emerson exclaims.[1] And tools represent labor. They make man aware of his work and the value of his work. The great development of ever more precise machine tools, the Industrial Revolution makes man self-conscious about the problems of labor.

Work, psychologically conceived, suggests the idea of play. From childhood on work and play are inseparably linked together in man's mind; and although their specific form and appearance may be multifarious in daily life, children and adults alike experience their existence in a steadfast rhythm which they recognize as tension and relaxation, work and play. Thus it is hardly surprising to find that the nineteenth century is also the age of play. Following Schiller's pioneering study of 1795,[2] a great number of theories appear, speculating on the nature of play. Clearly this is immediately related to the development of the study of psychology, which in turn runs parallel with the increasing importance of education in nineteenth-century society. Educational psychology is interested in play in the same way as that other characteristic nineteenth-century science, political economy, is interested in the nature of labor.

While the notions of play and work have thus received their fully detailed treatment as separate factors in the social structure, the question is still open as to how they relate mutually within the historical development of culture. Both play and labor are projections of man's inner being and by expressing themselves in distinct forms, they contribute the most authentic features of a culture. Culture is not play exclusively, nor work exclusively, but a configuration of the combined effects of play and labor factors. Questioning the similarities and dissimilarities of both is to examine the structure of historical society. To analyze the characteristics of labor and play in their separate and mutual aspects, and to trace their unmistakable social affinity, is fundamentally to reveal the inner fabric of culture itself.

1. MAN AND WORK

We all know and think we understand the meaning of work. Yet the definitions with which the theorists provide us leave the innocent worker highly confused. The idea of labor seems to be differently interpreted from mind to mind, and that this should be so is not surprising, and ought not to worry us. For an activity which is so closely connected with

[1] Emerson, "Society and Solitude", *Coll. Works*, Riverside Ed., VII, 151.
[2] Schiller, *Über die aesthetische Erziehung des Menschen.*

man's inner being must needs convey strong subjective connotations when put into formal expressions. If we find striking contrasts in the evaluation of labor by different authors, this presumably indicates a heavy stress on the emotional contents of the respective definitions. Thus when one expert explains that labor involves pain,[3] and another that labor and joy are tightly interwoven,[4] our attention is in both cases drawn to the results or the by-products of labor without receiving much information about its essential meaning.

Work reduced to its most simple and basic form is an encounter of the subject with the phenomenal world whereby an activity takes place which manipulates or controls certain objects. "All work is the conquering of objects", according to Eisler's *Wörterbuch der philosophischen Begriffe*. In its most general sense, that is according to the physical laws which include the application to mechanical equipment, it is the product of distance and force (p x s). But if one limits oneself to human activities, another essential element must be added in this conquest of objects, namely the transference of a part of the subjective self. Hegel views labor (like language) as an expression whereby the individual, as it were, is turned inside out and loses himself in another being.[5] In fact, the subject loses itself in the objectivity as THING,[6] and in this activity the individual satisfies the need for the 'pure destruction' of an object.

Historically, also, the conception of work shows a variety of evaluations. From age to age its practical meaning alters and widens (or narrows) according to the cultural development of man. This is already reflected in etymological derivations such as the German equivalent *Arbeit* from the Indo-Germanic *ar* 'to plow' (Greek *aroō*, Latin *arare*, Old-German *arjan*). Originally confined to a specific agricultural activity, the notion of labor comes to include all mental and physical work performed by man to fulfill his daily needs and those of society.

Although the notion of work does not figure prominently in any system of philosophy prior to Hegel, the religious and social importance of labor have been man's concern throughout the history of Western civilization. And since this is a Christian civilization, we may as well

---

[3] A. T. H(adley), in Baldwin's *Dictionary of Phil. & Psych.*
[4] J. Žmavc, "Elemente einer allgemeinen Arbeitstheorie", *Berner Studien zur Philosophie und ihrer Geschichte*, Band 48, p. 51, 1906.
[5] Hegel, *Phänomenologie des Geistes*, V.A.C.
[6] Hegel, "Jenenser Realphilosophie", *Sämtliche Werke* (Leipzig, 1932), XX, 197: "Arbeit ist das diesseitige Sich-zum-Dinge-Machen."

start by realizing that the religious interpretation of daily toil, which Christianity has inherited from Judaism, is based on punishment. Because of Adam's sin, according to the Genesis story, man is henceforth cursed and doomed to eat his bread in the sweat of his face. Thus labor and sorrow become almost identical in the Old Testament; the Book of Ecclesiastics is a continuous lamentation of the futility of man's work: "Then I looked on all the works that my hands had wrought . . . and behold, all was vanity and vexation of spirit." [7] The New Testament, though accepting the same premise, is less explicit in this gloom. It holds out the hope that man's labor will be redeemed through the mediacy of Christ, so that he may enter into an eternal rest.[8]

In practice, however, historical Christianity shows no implications of this conception of punishment, and by the time of the Reformation it provides theories which place labor more conveniently in the framework of human life, without, however, refuting the curse of Genesis. We cannot enter into the complicated problem of whether Luther's introduction of the German word *Beruf*, indicating an ambiguity of profession and calling, is theoretically or even linguistically correct. But his historic decision to translate the Greek *ponos* with *Beruf* demonstrates the necessity of coming to terms at that time with the exigencies of terrestrial society and making a frank pronouncement about Christian duties in an age when the process of secularization is in full swing. For if the original sin causes the alienation of man from God, exemplified in human toil, how can this daily recurring punishment be made understood as something more than a negative burden? By adding to the negative meaning the dimension of 'calling', Luther makes work an act of brotherly love. This is a stroke of genius, but the Lutheran stress on the individual and his personal salvation makes anything like what we call 'social service' ambiguous. Thus Calvin, with more practical sense, later slightly adjusts this view-point. In his daily work, man fulfills his duty towards society, but not for society's sake, but for the greater glory of God. In this sense human toil is transformed from sorrow to worship.[9]

[7] *Eccle.* 2: 11.
[8] *Math.* 11: 28, 29. *Hebr.* 4: 11.
[9] Therefore the greater the work the greater the glory of God? But the incentive in practice points clearly to material profit. And although Max Weber's thesis, based on the correlation between the Protestant ethic and the rise of capitalism has been refuted either entirely or in part, by scholars such as Martin, Tawney, Hyma and Brentano, there is no denying, to say the least, that the emphasis on the importance of hard work accelerated a development which had started modestly before the Reformation.

In all this, labor is regarded *sub specie aeternitatis*, but by the middle
of the eighteenth century, the secularization of life is so far advanced
that the theological interpretation of man and society loses its sway
altogether. The perspective of an hereafter disappears from human life,
at least in the thinking of the most representative spokesmen of the age,
and human happiness is no longer thought of in terms of salvation,
redemption, or God's glorification. Property, opulence, and comfort
are replacing them. The measure of man's well-being, according to
Adam Smith, lies in the extent to which he can "enjoy the necessaries,
conveniences and amusements of human life".[10] Man is rich or poor
according to the quantity of labor which he either commands or can
afford to purchase. "The value of any commodity therefore, to the
person who possesses it, and who means not to use or consume it
himself, but to exchange it for other commodities, is equal to the quantity of labor which it enables him to purchase or command." [11] Thus
human work in the political-economical view is linked exclusively with
commodities, that is objects: self-interest drives man to conquer, purchase or command a thing-world. And (although Smith does not draw
this conclusion) in this way the subject loses itself in the world of
objects, an objectivation which, as we shall see below, lies at the bottom
of Hegel's idea of alienation.

Adam Smith, although clearly the oracle of the bourgeois man of
property, is with his conviction that labor represents the only universal
and accurate measure of value, and "the only standard by which we
can compare the values of different commodities of all times and all
places",[12] nevertheless the true teacher of the Marxists. His views also
make a great impression on Hegel, who bases his subtle reflections
on the division of labor on Smith's well-known example of pin-making.[13]
Hegel's pre-occupation with the philosophical explanation of work constitutes one of the major contributions to nineteenth-century social
thinking, without which hardly any other theory of labor-relations can
be evaluated. Already in his lectures at the University of Jena in the
period from 1803-1806, he tackled the problem of labor, bringing it
under the dialectical scheme of subject and object with the self-sure
argumentation which is never to leave him.

Labor, to Hegel, is the mediator between man and his world. It

[10]   Adam Smith, *Wealth of Nations*, I, 5.
[11]   *Ibid.*
[12]   *Ibid.*
[13]   *Ibid.*, I, 1.

creates the unity between the individual and the phenomenon as it stands in the middle of a relationship in which the subject tries to destroy the object.[14] At the root of all labor is need, and the satisfaction of this need as 'movement' and mediation, destroys the object. Things are worked upon and changed (verarbeitet), "their inner universal potentiality is put in an outer form".[15]

The invention of tools, culminating in the machine, has moved man away from nature without, however, taking from him the fundamental need of work. Thus he cheats nature. With the machine man practises a deception (Betrug) on nature in-as-much as the destruction of the object is perpetrated indirectly without suspending the need for labor. But although this makes his life more comfortable, essentially he loses out. He loses contact with nature, he does not approach nature as a living being any longer, and the work which is still left to him has become mechanical, an abstract and outward activity.[16] In the world of the factory, labor thus becomes an abstract general activity; that is, the individual does not satisfy his own particular needs, but is a part in a totality of needs. His dexterity limited, labor to him is absolutely dead, and the consciousness of the laborer degenerates to its ultimate level of bluntness.[17]

This concern with the abstraction of work in the mechanical age reappears in Hegel's later works. In the Encyklopädie der philosophischen Wissenschaften the division of labor is seen as the result of the process of mechanization. Abstracted labor leads on the one hand to lighter work and greater production, but on the other to a limitation of human skill. Skill itself becomes mechanical in this manner and is "the ability to replace human work by the machine".[18] Again in

---

[14] Hegel, Jenenser Realphil. S.W., 19, 220. Georg Simmel, Philosophie des Geldes (Leipzig, 1900), 484, in his view that the division of labor is caused by the separation of objective and subjective culture, follows Hegel in this matter.
[15] Hegel, S.W., 20, 214.
[16] Hegel, S.W., 19, 237, S.W., 20, 215. Walter Rathenau sees in mechanical labor an evil as such which constitutes the central problem for socialism, a problem "which neither Marx nor Lenin can solve". Die neue Gesellschaft, 1923, p. 75. See also Kritik der Zeit, 76.
[17] Hegel, S.W., 19, 239. Concern with the deterioration of the mind as a result of industrialization, is also reflected in the educational thoughts of Pestalozzi: especially in "Ueber Volksbindung und Industrie", Ges. Werke (Zurich, 1946), he deplores factory work with its routine mechanism of isolated skills which has a detrimental effect on man (VII, 441) and proposes a plan for an elementary industrial education with the object not only of cultivating the human mind, but also of 'humanizing' industry (VII, 456).
[18] Hegel, Enc., 525, 526.

his work on the philosophy of law, Hegel emphasizes that the price of greater production is the abstraction of man's natural needs into a mechanical existence in which factory equipment replaces his immediate contact with nature.[19]

The pivotal point in Hegel's analysis of labor is evidently this objectivation (*das Sich-zum-Dinge-Machen*) of man's consciousness. In the process of work the human self becomes abstract and generalized; it turns its inner potentiality outside and thus alienates (*entäussert*) itself. In the Jena lectures Hegel does not explicitly link alienation with labor; [20] this is to come in his *Phenomenologie*. But from what has been said above it is clear that to Hegel any human work is caught in the dialectic of the human subjectivity negating the object, and the consciousness of the objective world negating the self-consciousness of the individual. As such, all labor, in the objectivation of the self, represents alienation because it transfers something of the inner self to the object, where it gets lost and becomes thing.

Marx's thoughts on alienation are, in principle at least, truly Hegelian. But when it comes to the application of this idea to labor, there emerges a characteristic difference. In Hegel's interpretation, the objectivation by which the consciousness loses itself in the thing-world, is an inevitable alienation belonging to man's essential nature. It can only be suspended (*aufgehoben*) in the idea of philosophy, the absolute Spirit. But this line of thought is objectionable to Marx.[21] The absolute Spirit is a mystification altogether. And the abstraction of his human dignity which the laborer suffers in an industrial society is by no means inevitable but caused by a concrete evil: the capitalist system. In his economic-philosophical manuscript of 1844 Marx gives the clearest exposition of his views on this matter. In the bourgeois system the laborer has become a commodity, the most miserable commodity of all.[22] He has sold his work to a production system in which his human interest is nil and his human dignity is crushed. Instead of expressing (*äusseren*) his individuality in society, his individuality is alienated (*entäussert*). He is a part of the machinery without having a share in the profits of its

---

[19] *Grundlinien der Philosophie d. Rechts*, 196, 198.
[20] The word *entäussert* appears only twice, but it is here, under the heading *Constitution*, exclusively related to the alienation of the individual for the sake of the general will. Vol. 20, 242-245.
[21] For a thorough treatment of the differences between the views of Hegel and Marx in matters of labor, see Georg Lukács, *Der junge Hegel* (Wien, 1948), 699, 705, and the entire chapter "Die Entäusserung".
[22] Marx, *Frühe Schriften* (Stuttgart, 1962), I, 550.

production. His alienation, however, can be overcome through a radical social revolution whereby the proletariat destroys the capitalist system and seizes the production apparatus for the benefit of man's integrity. This destruction is part and parcel of the Hegelian dialectic, but modifies Hegel's suspension significantly and places the dialectic logic in the stream of nineteenth-century nihilism.[23]

Whereas Hegel sees the problem of labor and alienation ontologically, relating it to the problem of man's inner being, for Marx it is limited to an economic-political issue.[24] Kierkegaard, in his own dialectical treatment regards labor, however, as a foremost ethical problem, which results from the dualism of the esthetic and ethical needs of the mind. He is personally involved in this antinomy, as he works frantically on his books, while, however, living on a private fortune which releases him from toil for daily bread. This is a sincere concern to him, expressed in many of his works, but clarified in the most articulate terms in his *Either-Or*. In his analysis the idea of duty is central to the understanding of work. For on the esthetic level the 'duty to work for a living' is a limitation of the individual's freedom, and the esthete scoffs at duty as a pedestrian activity which obliterates the refined pleasures of life. But on the ethical level, duty is a moral imperative, expressing what is universally human and as such representing a manifestation of freedom. "By working man frees himself, by working he becomes the ruler of nature, by working he proves that he is higher than nature".[25] In this sense, and in strong contrast to Marx's views, all work, even the most abstracted and alienated, satisfies human dignity. The joy and beauty of work can be experienced only in a moral disposition, regardless of the nature and scope of the labor involved.

Kierkegaard's ascetic solution of the problem lies beyond the alternative blessing or curse, which in the nineteenth century plays a remarkable role because it occurs outside the traditional theological context.

---

[23] Karl Löwith, *Von Hegel bis Nietzsche* (Zürich, 1944), 381. According to Heinrich Popitz, *Der entfremdete Mensch* (Basel, 1953), 112, there are basically two motifs in Marx's work: the exposition of the alienation of modern man and the foundation of his rehabilitation, the *Aneignung*, through revolution. The history of mankind to Marx represents the antithesis of alienation (the preparing phase) and truth (the realization), p. 165.

[24] In the *Capital* the word alienation does not occur, but the idea is clearly present in Marx's exposition of the Fetishism of commodities (I.I.4). In the sense that Marx applies it to labor and commodities only, Sidney Hook in his Introduction to *From Hegel to Marx* is correct in saying that the idea of alienation is foreign to Marx's conception of man.

[25] Kierkegaard, *Samlede Vaerker* (Copenhagen, 1962), III, 260.

The Victorian glorification of work as a 'blessing', brought out in the work of such otherwise utterly contrasting authors as Carlyle and Zola for instance, is neither socially nor religiously conceived. Such is Arnold Ruge's interpretation which regards labor as a divine, creative principle in world history, making the human being into real man.[26] Over against this stands Nietzsche's denunciation of labor. There is no satisfaction in work; on the contrary, his belief in vital joy makes him reject the idea of daily toil as a blessing. Work is a curse. A curse, however, not derived from an original sin, but a self-inflicted misery in the life of modern man. Leaving himself no time for the enjoyment of reflection, he rushes from place to place, filling his time with countless activities, as he hunts for wealth and property, thereby killing forms and ceremonies of a cultured life as well as any expression of his inner being. Here the alienation shows up clearly in the feverish compulsion to be busy, thus replacing the basic urge to satisfy common and communal needs which come in a rhythm of concentration and relaxation. For this corruption Nietzsche blames the American way of life which demonstrates a 'wildness characteristic of the blood of the Red Indians' in the way people rush for gold and in the breathless hurry of their work.[27]

Blessing and curse do not pose a choice according to Berdyaev, for they form the double aspect of the redemption which is, or should be, characteristic of labor. If man is essentially alienated, he can redeem himself in his daily work. But as far as this constitutes a moral problem, no economic theory has as yet shown any concern about it, and for this reason Berdyaev attacks both the bourgeois and socialist systems. The capitalist aims to preserve that form of slavery which he hypocritically calls 'free labor', and the socialist strives for freedom from labor and ignores the creativity of work.[28] Berdyaev knows from personal experience that the alienation of the worker as it has grown up under capitalist exploitation, is not remedied in communist state systems, and that the restoration (*Aneignung*) of the worker to the totality of human dignity, which according to the Marxists is to occur after the proletarian revolution, is not being realized there. But his voice, speaking from an orthodox but rather abstract Christian conviction, is merely an echo of the past and seems somewhat out of place among the more radical and forceful pronouncements of the socialist and communist doctrines, or of Nietzsche's *Lebensphilosophie*.

[26] Löwith, 269-271.
[27] Nietzsche, *Fröhliche Wissenschaft*, Aph. 329.
[28] Berdyaev, *Destiny of Man*, II, iv, 7.

In the twentieth century perhaps the most radical and forceful pro-nouncement on the laborer comes from a man who, although in the Vitalist tradition of the Will to Power, defies Nietzsche's contempt of pedestrian toil and proclaims the working man as the future Superman. In Ernst Jünger's conception the Worker is the technocratic hero and the soldier of the future. This figure is the obvious product of a highly emotional mind exacerbated by the terrors of war. In *Der Arbeiter* (1932) Jünger declares that man can assert himself only if he plays the game of technology, otherwise he will go under.[29] What nature was to him in previous ages, the technical world is to him now. The great slogan is TOTAL MOBILIZATION, for war will not be the exception, but the norm, and here the worker-technocrat will be the leading hero. Jünger is by no means a National-socialist,[30] but it is not surprising to find the Hitler government buying and reprinting his works for propaganda. Their irrational climate and style can easily be made misunderstood. This emotional and martial conception of labor, for all its emphasis on technology, is at the opposite pole to the cold scientific interpretation of a previous generation, for instance in the work of William Ostwald, where labor and culture are explained as mere physical energy.[31]

Jünger's conclusions can hardly be taken as representative of our age; yet his works, conceived in the climate of war, death, violence, anxiety and technology, appeal to the basic emotions of the time. His im-portance lies in the fact that he recognizes the fundamental events and problems of the twentieth century, and this makes him one of the most typical spokesman of his generation.[32] In Jünger's presentation of the Worker, the idea of labor has reached the ultimate climax of alienation. The problem of pleasure-in-work (*Arbeitsfreude*) which to Jaspers has become insoluble,[33] because the man is separated from the

---

[29] Jünger, *Der Arbeiter* (Hamburg, 1932), 2nd ed., 158. *Technik* in Jünger's sense is absolutely nihilistic. While in the bourgeois era it represents the organ of progress, in the technocratic age technique, "that is the mobilization through the Worker, is ... the disturber of all faith ... it negates in its sheer existence". (p. 154-156.)

[30] Jünger published a satirical novel on the Hitler régime: *On the Marble Cliffs* (1939).

[31] Ostwald, *Energetische Grundlagen der Kulturwissenschaft* (Leipzig, 1909). The work deals with the foundation of sociology from the point of view of Energetics, p. 3. Cf. also Oskar Nagel, *Die Welt als Arbeit* (Stuttgart, 1909).

[32] For the question whether or not Jünger really represents his age, see J. P. Stern, *Ernst Jünger* (New Haven, 1953), p. 17.

[33] Jaspers, *Geist. Situation d. Zeit* (Berlin, 1947), 5th ed., 52.

worker in the technocratic age, can be overcome only in the cynical *Kraft-durch-Freude* program of the Nazis. Here Jünger's ideas about total mobilization, though without his consent, receive their practical application.

In a brief survey like this a total picture of labor theories can obviously not be attempted; but even from this selection it seems clear that the historical development points to an ever greater awareness of the separation of individual and society. However great the differences between the various interpretations of labor may be, whether they are ontologically, politically, ethically, socially, or martially directed, the problem lies in the widening chasm between man and society. The alienation shows up in the decreasing enjoyment of work, running parallel with the growing mechanization; and indeed alienation of labor is exactly this loss of satisfaction, of vitality, of play. The power-through-joy formula for a smooth military machine of the Nazis is only its most hypocritical expression.

2. MAN AND PLAY

In the fifteenth letter of his *Esthetic Education*, Schiller declares that man is completely man only when he plays.[34] By this he means that man can fulfill his deep potential in the totality of culture only on the basis of play. We shall see below what his idea of play specifically entails. But it is clear that play in its most universal meaning is not accessory to life, but essential to the expression of our innermost self. This quality it shares with labor. It is an intrinsic urge which belongs to the creativity of the human psyche. It is fundamental in the development of culture.

But what is play essentially? Why do we play? Since the latter question is of less importance for us, it may be answered first. It reflects the bio-psychological aspect of the problem, and indispensable as this may be, it reveals little of the broader cultural implications. Schiller was the first to suggest an explanation in this sense. In the concluding letter of the same work, he thinks that play is caused by a SURPLUS of vital energy; "The animal works when he is driven by a need, and plays when driven by an abundance of energy, when an excessive vitality stimulates him to activity." This view, shared by the novelist Jean Paul and the Psychologist Beneke,[35] becomes popular

[34] Schiller, *Werke* (Horen-Ausgabe), XI, 57.
[35] Friedrich Beneke, *Empirical psychology as the basis of Knowledge* (1820).

through Herbert Spencer's *Principles of Psychology* (1855) in which he explains play as an overflow of energy.

The nineteenth century appears to be fond of speculating on the causes of play. Among the most famous of these theories is that of Karl Groos with his thorough-going analysis of the play of human beings as well as animals. To him it is chiefly a preparatory training for adult life: "The development of the individual to full manhood or womanhood by means of an allround exercise of his or her capacities." [36] Wilhelm Wundt in his *Vorlesungen über die Menschen- und Tierseele* recognizes the playful activities as IMITATION of purposeful acts of the will; [37] while the school of Lazarus produces the theory of RELAXA-TION,[38] Julius Schaller prefers to view play in connection with serious-ness: if play does not allow for serious elements, it will itself become a boring seriousness without content.[39]

With the twentieth century we arrive at the more fanciful interpreta-tions. There is, for instance, the PURGE theory by which an Aristotelian principle of tragedy is applied to play,[40] and the ATAVISTIC explanation which considers that play is a necessary exercise for the disappearance of rudimentary functions which have become useless.[41] This embarrass-ment of choices may incline one to doubt the validity of so many alternatives, and like Claparède, who is close to Groos, to dismiss most of them.[42] It is probably nearer to the truth to suggest, as Zondervan does, that each of these theories emphasizes only one aspect of play and that none deserves preference over the other.[43] Together they demonstrate the richness and width of the field in which play operates.

So much for the biological causes of play activity. What interests us more is the question as to what play actually represents in the relation-ship between man and society and the nature of its cultural function.

[36] Groos, *The Play of Man*, Transl. Elizabeth Baldwin (New York, 1901), 406. Konrad Lange, in *Das Wesen der Kunst* (Berlin, 1907), 2nd ed., sees in play not only a preparation, but also a further exercise, thus developing the completion theory.
[37] *Vorlesungen* . . . (Hamburg, 1906), 4th ed., 427.
[38] Lazarus, *Über die Reize des Spiels* (Berlin, 1883), While refuting Pascal's idea that play is an escape, Lazarus sees in it an elevating relaxation (*erhebende Erholung*), p. 51.
[39] Schaller, *Das Spiel und die Spiele* (Weimar, 1861), p. 100.
[40] Harvey A. Carr, *The Survival Values of Play* (Boulder, Colorado, 1902).
[41] For instance represented by Stanly Hall, *Adolescence* (London, 1904), and *Ped. Sem.*, IX, 1902.
[42] Edouard Claparède, *Psychologie de l'Enfant* (Genève, 1911), 4th ed., 166 ff.
[43] H. Zondervan, *Het spel bij dieren, kinderen en volwassen menschen* (Amster-dam, 1928), 58.

The obvious characteristics are self-evident: play produces the feeling of enjoyment, of freedom; it means relaxation. But the enjoyment is never divorced from seriousness, the freedom is bound by strict rules, and the relaxation counter-acted by intense concentration. These well-known aspects of play, which we can observe daily in children and animals, do not need further elaboration. They serve to emphasize, however, that play is self-contradictory. It binds and frees, it moves and concentrates, it is tense and it is relaxed at the same time.

The varieties of play are staggering, and the experts such as Groos, Schaller, Claparède, and Zondervan, produce elaborate classifications of distinct forms. It is clearly obligatory to recognize the difference between the expression of play, for instance, in children's games, primitive rites, the Roman *ludi*, or in theatre performances. But in order to understand what it is that unites these multifarious modes in the cultural pattern, we must look for a basic principle which can explain how the individual play activity may transcend and become a function in the development of civilization. This, I believe, must be seen in the exchange which is inherent in all play. In play the common value by which we recognize things is exchanged for an imaginary one. Make-believe is fundamental. When children arrange chairs in a straight line and call it a train, the common value of the chairs is transformed into a play-value which, as long as the game lasts, is just as real as the original. The bird or fish mask which the primitive tribesman wears in his ritual dance, has lost its material value and IS the demon to whom the sacred cult is devoted. Similarly, the symbols of Judaism and Christianity represent in concrete forms something else that is too sacred and mysterious to grasp in its immediacy. Here emerges the symbolic nature of all play. It appears to be rooted in the polarity between a meaning and an image which is sustained in an illusion. Indeed, play is ILLUSION, that is literally in-playing in an understood exchange of substance and appearance. It is strongly evident in those games which can be classified as contests. In sport games, for instance, there is always the imagined enemy; without the feeling of the presence of an enemy the game would collapse. This idea of *agon* has a long history which again originates from sacred ceremonies.

Greek civilization is permeated with this AGONAL feeling, as Burckhardt is the first to discover.[44] The Greeks organize contests wherever

[44] Burckhardt, *Griechische Kulturgeschichte* (Berlin, 1931), XI, 47. Huizinga has demonstrated that this is not, as Burckhardt thinks, an exclusive feature of Greek culture and that we now, with our greater knowledge of anthropology,

they see a possibility: at symposia, while drinking or eating, in sports or theatre performances. The sacred character, however, is here definitely retained. Sport games and drama continue to manifest their religious origins until the Roman professional moves in. No religion can have an impact without an arch-foe. In the struggle for life and death, insofar as reflected in sports and theatre play, the 'enemy' is crucial. But the fact that he is at the same time real and imagined, provides play with its typical nature.

It would appear that play is fundamentally a polar relationship of contrasting elements which negate and stimulate each other. Appearance and substance, pseudo and original form, are never entirely lost for each other. The doll and the human being which it represents must both needs retain their reality, or the illusion is destroyed. In sports the feeling of friendship and animosity both remain essential, or there can be no game. Without this creative moment of reciprocal affirming and negating, of aggression and withdrawal, of concentration and yielding, the nature of play cannot be recognized. Its polarity is already expressed in the etymological derivations of the word. Play, from the Anglo-Saxon root *plega*, early indicates a fast and repetitive movement, up and down, back and forth. There are overtones of battle and war, as well as love.[45] In Middle-Dutch works such as *Hadewych, Beatrys, Esmoreit*, the word *spelen* may thus mean the act of love.

So far we have dealt with play as an autonomous unity, the game as enjoyed according to certain pre-arranged rules. It is clear, however, that in the development of culture self-contained games as such do not contribute to classical achievement. The work of great artists, generals, or philosophers does not represent a series of games, not even of a sublime order. But it does manifest a highly developed ELEMENT of play which is distinct from the element of labor. A musical composition or a painting is not play in the psychological or biological sense, but the creative activity which produces them seems to be subject to the same laws as play. There is order and freedom, concentration and relaxation, dead seriousness and enjoyment.

The importance of play for social and educational purposes has, of course, been reflected upon during the ages. In the seventh book of

---

may conclude that the *agon* appears universally in ancient civilization. *Homo ludens: proeve eener bepaling van het spel-element der cultuur* (Haarlem, 1938), 103 ff.

[45] See for further etymological data the interesting, but unnecessarily extended treatment in Huizinga, *op. cit.*, 40-66.

his Laws Plato confirms the religious roots as well as purposes of play in life. Aristotle deems play important, but only as an opportunity for rest. For "play is not an end, it only exists for the sake of activity".[46] These are, however, casual observations, not embedded in a system. Detailed thinking about the function of play in society comes more than ten centuries later. Not even the educators devote much attention to it, although Jan Amos Comenius, in the seventeenth century, believes that school exercises may be given in the form of games, and in fact, tries to realize this.[47]

It is not until the eighteenth century that we can find a definite awareness of the importance of the play factor for cultural achievement. Kant, in his *Critique of Jugdment*, uses the word *Spiel* when classifying the arts according to philosophical judgments: the rhetorical, the plastic (*bildende*) and those of the play of sentiments.[48] The confusion which this classification produces seems to result mainly from an absence of a clearly delineated notion of play. Kant uses the word repeatedly, but chiefly as a means of distinguishing various kinds of esthetic judgments and their objects, not as a tool to understand how the arts function in society. Nor does he attempt to probe into the nature of play itself.

This is first undertaken by Schiller. Schiller knows the *Critique of Judgment* well and in his letters on *Esthetic Education* he sets out to put the idea of play in a logical system. He is no trained philosopher and has by no means the penetrating analytical power of Kant's mind. But as a poet and playwright he has the advantage of knowing the creative process of artistic achievement at first hand, and moreover, shows a sustained sense of culture in its historical totality. At the roots of all play are two drives, the 'urge of nature' (*Stofftrieb*) and the 'urge of reason' (*Formtrieb*). The object of the first, which is a sensate drive, is called life in its widest sense, while the object of the second is called form.[49] These two urges Schiller recognizes as antithetical, in the sense that they negate, but also stimulate each other to a higher comprehensive synthesis which he calls 'living form'. The living form is nothing else but what we understand as symbol. It reflects man's need to express

---

[46]   *Eth. Nic.*, X, 6, 6.
[47]   Comenius' *Schola ludus seu Encyclopedia viva* ..., is a dramatization in 5 acts, 21 scenes and 52 dramatis personae, aiming at presenting the natural facts of the world in play form.
[48]   *Urtheilskraft*, II, § 51.
[49]   Schiller, *Werke* (HA), XI, 53. Croce also regards play not as an activity in itself, but rather as an alternating of contrasting, vital impulses: "I piaceri dell' imaginazione", *Frammenti di Etica*, XV, Bari, 1922.

his inner self in concrete image, and to objectivate in more or less adequate forms his subjective experiences.

The importance of this interpretation lies in the fact that for the first time it points out the inherent dialectic in play and its symbolizing quality in the framework of culture. Dialectic is of course something different from polarity, which we noted in play while describing it above as separate games. Polarity is a physical phenomenon which cannot properly be transferred to logic and the product of polarity is not a synthesis in the formal sense. But the symbolizing act which expresses itself in an organic form is to Schiller the logical synthesis of the contrasting relationship between sensate and intelligent forces.[50] Play also distinguishes itself essentially from work in the symbol, as we shall see further on.

In the nineteenth and twentieth centuries the theories of play acquire a more anthropological character. Burckhardt, as we have noted, stresses the AGONAL element in ancient Greek civilization, especially after the heroic age, an element which Huizinga is to take up later and elaborate, in a more general sense. In Schiller's theories the Greek achievements are also central in that they give the example for the unity and harmony which play alone can provide, but they touch on the idea of contest only in passing. With the advance of anthropology in the nineteenth century, however, more and more material becomes available to demonstrate that most, if not all, cultures know the prize-fight and the ceremonial battle in relationship to their sacred cult, and the accent on the evaluation of play moves to the contest-element.

According to Frobenius, who studies primitive cultures in Africa,[51] primitive man, in his sacred cults and dances, plays the order of nature as it has become conscious to him in the rhythm of life and death, of ripening and withering, of summer and winter. Although differing from Frobenius in some conclusions, Huizinga follows this up and with the help of much anthropological data, gives a description of the various aspects of play in the historical development of civilizations, thereby leaning heavily on the *agon*, the *wedkamp*, the contest. He has little interest in the symbolic nature of play and mentions it only casually. For instance, in the pages on play and poetry [52] there is only a hint at

---

[50]   We cannot here enter into Schiller's application of 'esthetic' play to the problem of moral freedom and to a possible 'esthetic state' in which a complete harmony between man and society is achieved in absolute freedom.

[51]   Frobenius, *Kulturgeschichte Afrikas* (Phaidon, 1933).

[52]   Huizinga, *op. cit.*, 170-195. The historian Eduard Meyer points to the relationship of art and play in his *Geschichte des Altertums* (Basel, 1953), 6th ed.,

the representative value of play; most of them deal with literary contests, with poetical games and technical rules. In Schiller's theory we find a firm logical principle of unity, explaining the harmony of the creative process and the function of play in society, but it has a limited value in our time because the esthetic, political and social implications are dated for us. On the other hand, in the anthropological interpretations the underlying principle is weak or lacking, but we are given a wealth of descriptive details of the outward aspects of play.

3. MAN AND CULTURE

Labor and play when closely examined appear to be very much alike. Naturally, in the daily circumstances of our existence we experience them emotionally as contrasts. Thus it is said that play is free, work compulsory. But a closer look reveals that the freedom of play is conditioned by strict rules which in their disciplines are just as compulsory as the rules of labor. And who would deny that much work can be done in pleasure and freedom, through the responsibility of choice in matters of management, design or organization? It is true that there is conspicuously little freedom for the worker at the conveyor-belt, but there certainly is a fair amount in the planning and organization of the assembly line. We should therefore not confuse abstracted (alienated) toil, which is basically slave-labor, with healthy creative work.

Again, it is said that labor is strenuous and heavy, while play is relaxing and light. That labor is serious and play fun.[53] But this can be only a superficial characterization. Fifteen minutes of fencing is more strenuous than two hours of roadwork. The play-element that everyone recognizes in the achievements of artists, composers or poets, does not make their work lighter and indeed, they rarely seem to be the most relaxed members of society. It seems therefore necessary to avoid making judgments on the basis of emotional notions and external evidence, or misleading confusions will result.[54] Much confusion may be eliminated if we recognize that there is an essential part of play in

---

167. Play is imporatnt for culture, for it is not only a copy (*Abbild*), but also a rudiment of a religious or political action.

[53] Lazarus, *op. cit.*, p. 15. Cf. Huizinga, *op. cit.*, 4, where the epithet *grap* (joke or fun) is used, rather misleadingly.

[54] For instance in Herbert Read's remark: "Play is freedom, is disinterestedness, and it is only by virtue of disinterested free activity that man has created his cultural values. Perhaps it is this theory of all work and no play that has made

work, and equally essential part of work in play. On this basis one can understand the similarities in both and consequently also that which distinguishes the two.

Play and work are man's most essential and authentic activity in which he directly or indirectly, consciously or unconsciously, expresses his inner being. This expressing is nothing but the transfer of subjectivity to the world of objects. In both play and labor the individual loses a part of his subjective self in the OTHER, the world of things. What the tool is to the laborer the toy is to the playing child; they are both objectivations of the individual urge, experience or need. This is true from the most elementary activities to the most skillful forms of labor and sports. In this sense the borderline between work and play becomes almost impossible to draw, for the awareness of life, be it in work or play, is fixed in the dialectic relationship of Self and phenomenon, and indeed, "man plays his full existence in the rapport between two contrasting and inseparable terms: the I and the non-I".[55] In this relationship intensity plays a decisive role. The quality of work and play is immediately contingent on the concentration of energy by which the subjectivity is transformed into object. Genius is commonly said to be a capacity for great concentration and hard labor. But the less conspicuous artist or scholar also knows the intensity of concentration which is needed to give concrete shape to his experience, ideas, or imagination. The demarcation line, again, is here impossible to define. Who in the final accomplishment can with any measure of certainty describe where in a work of art, poetry or music, the element of labor ends and that of play begins?

Finally, if the experiences of work and play are indeed so fundamentally alike, it must be asked whether the self-alienation which, as we noted, is so central in the theories of labor, should not similarly apply to the realm of play. The answer requires some care. If we understand the word alienation, as some popular sociologists do, to be the sorry plight of unfortunate citizens in their social environment, caused for instance, by a wrong distribution of labor, then the conclusion must be negative. Nobody can be imagined to suffer from play. But we must take the term in its relation to the total cultural manifestation of a nation or an era. If we use the term in its most general form, as Hegel does, and

---

the Marxist such a very dull boy." *Existentialism, Marxism, and Anarchism* (London, 1949), p. 14. This is a misrepresentation of play, of culture and of Marxism as well.

[55] Jeanne Hersch, *L'Être et la Forme* (Genève, 1946), 21.

regard it as any objectivation of the self, then from what has been said above, it follows that all play, by its very nature, is an expression or alienation. In this present context a few examples of play-alienation may suffice.

In the Olympic games, from their founding in 776 B.C. when they are still very much incorporated in the cultic organization, until Hellenistic times when the element of nationalistic glory is added, the characteristics of play are unquestionable. With Roman supremacy, however, the original nature changes and the athlete becomes PROFESSIONAL, that is a part of the commercial system: sport deteriorates into trade. What happens here, essentially, is not a decline as such. For it can easily be argued that the professional improves the virtuosity of the game and breaks more records. The important thing is that the original quality of play, for whatever it is worth, is given up for a commercial one. Play indeed has become labor.

In the realm of art no one can fail to see the inherent freedom of play which determines the ultimate form of a painting, or a piece of sculpture. This is directly related to the artist's personal style, the originality with which he handles the material. The search for originality and the effort to demonstrate it, have, since the days of the Romantic movement, their own history, into which we cannot here probe. But the galleries of contemporary art show us ample evidence that what was at first a natural and often unconscious expression of the artist's inner personality has now become a deliberate and almost mechanical device. The personal touch has become a rubber stamp, often cunningly planned to attract a large public, or rather the dealers and galleries. Not long ago, I visited a painter, whom I knew as a competent artist of landscapes in attractive, but fairly conventional style. To my surprise I found in his studio, piled on top of each other, large canvases representing the same scene; pollarded willows, semi-abstracted into geometrical patterns. When I raised my eyebrows, he explained that his agent wanted him to have a trade-mark, and from now on he was to paint geometrically distorted willows with persistent conformity, and only slight allowance for variation. This is as we know, fairly representative for much that is going on in contemporary art. The expression of the artist's personality, that is his objectivation in forms, has lost its quality of play and becomes a commercial gimmick, a trade-mark indeed.

But what about the DIFFERENCE between play and work? For, after all, granted that the two have much in common, and even have the same organic structure, we do recognize them practically speaking as contrasts. If, as we have seen in the foregoing, the play-element in sports and in art can change into that of labor, a clear distinction is already implicit.

There IS, of course, a cardinal difference between play and labor. But it does not lie in emotions such as freedom, pleasure, or strain. It does not lie primarily in the activity itself of the individual involved in either labor or play. The difference, it seems to me, manifests itself chiefly in the result of these activities. Play and labor are not only a matter of the individual whose personality, in objectivation, is transferred to the forms of play and labor, they are also, and in the light of culture, foremost a concern of the 'other' world outside his own: society. The moment an individual act of labor or play is completed, it is outside the subject; its result is public domain. It may in a sense seem to belong to him, yet it is publicized, that is, submitted to public judgment. But once brought 'into the open' labor and play exercise a different effect on society. Both may be experienced in pleasure and both may convey pleasure to others. Labor, however, results in a product, with an immediate use and market value, whereas the meaning of play is entirely absorbed in its symbolizing performance. Dilthey, discussing the relationship between work and play, remarks that work aims at a concrete result, lying outside the actual activity whereas play finds its satisfaction in the activity itself.[56] Work knows a pre-arranged purpose; play, if it has one at all, is unconscious of it. Work is immediately appropriated by society, even if the product cannot be sold for awhile, for it is made to fit society's needs. Play, on the contrary, is not planned to be useful, it may only indirectly, by accident, become so. For instance, children's play is autonomous in itself, but is can under certain circumstances, produce pedagogic theories. Ball games originally belong to the players, but they can, as they have done, develop into shows for spectators.

From this vantage-point we are able to see the importance of both the play factor and the labor factor in the cultural development. We are inclined to give our full attention to the 'playfulness' of great civilizations, as Schiller, Burckhardt and Huizinga have done. This is not surprising, in view of the fact that herein are expressed the most characteristic features of cultural varieties and artistic styles. Ortega y Gasset, however, hints at the importance of work for culture when he

[56] Dilthey, *Ges. Schr.*, IX, 206.

says that "the necessity and obligations of culture impose on humanity the execution of certain tasks. The effort that is made to complete them is accordingly compulsory. This compulsory effort, imposed for the sake of pre-determined ends, is work." [57] For the full appreciation, however, of culture in its totality and subsequently in its process of alienation, it seems necessary not to overlook the way the labor factor is interlocked with that of play.

We have already noticed how in a work of art, the borderline between the two is often impossible to draw. A portrait insofar as it is commissioned, will represent a good deal of labor, and the artist will work with the feeling of duty and responsibility that goes with labor. But insofar as the finished product is not so much a certain likeness of the person who posed for it, but foremost an expression of what the artist imagined about that person, the painting will show elements lying outside the technique of mere copying, which we recognize as elements of play. They manifest the same purposeless nature, the same 'innocence', the same selfconcentration as a child's game.

The difference between the useful and the symbolizing act must naturally vary according to the manifold types of cultural expressions. In drama the factor of immediate usefulness is clearly evident in that it is planned for the stage. Most successful plays have been written for a particular company, whether it be the Dionysian festivals, the company of Richard Burbage, the Weimar Court theatre, Antoine's *Théâtre libre* or Strindberg's *Intima Teatern*. But drama would be merely a consumer product if it did not also carry a symbolic meaning within it. It 'represents' something, the inner meaning of the age as experienced and usually unconsciously and innocently brought out by the playwright, whereby drama becomes that characteristic mirror and representation of life, the *imitatio vitae, speculum consuetudinis* in Cicero's words.

We by no means have to confine ourselves, however, to the most brilliant accomplishments of civilization, such as we find in the arts and literature. Even on the most routine level of daily existence the saleability of labor cannot be divorced from the play-factor in society. Our eating and drinking, for instance, occurs, without our being aware of it, with all the rules, ceremonies and purposeless paraphernalia which we can recognize, if we stop to think, as typical for play. For our mere sustenance it would suffice to lap our food from the plate, or to be

[57] Ortega y Gasset, *The Modern Theme*, transl. J. Cleugh (1961), 82.

even more straight-forward, to munch the roots and fruits in the bush like the aboriginal gatherer. With the historical development of our tastes, however, we have invented ceremonies by which, unlike the animal, we eat in company, very much as in the pre-arranged game. We have come to believe that these forms are essential, but this is only relatively so. The more or less elegant eating and drinking in company heighten the pleasures of social life, but by no means better satisfy our basic need for proteins and vitamins; on the contrary, they tend to over-supply them.

Here two observations must be made. First, the play factor in civilized eating and drinking produces a symbolizing action. The fundamentally purposeless gestures of handling fork and knife and of making a toast, as well of the ornamentation of crystal, damask, silver and porcelain REPRESENT something lying far outside the physiological need of eating. They are part of our means of communicating, like language in the conversation which civilized minds consider an important attribute of dining. They are signs of our relationship to the outside world and express among other things, the measure of our social prestige and status. Secondly, as far as work is concerned, it is clear that the labor which goes into the preparing and consuming of the Bushman's meal is considerably less than that required for let us say, a knightly banquet in the Middle Ages. But by comparison the total amount of labor involved in the dinner parties that enliven our age, is simply staggering, if we, as we should, include not only the elaborate cooking and processing of the food, but also the manufacturing of cutlery, stoves, refrigerators, and the ornamental trappings and trimmings that go with these occasions.

It would appear from this that as the play forms in society increase, the quantity of labor involved is proportionately larger. When religion moves out of the catacombs to chapels and thence to cathedrals, there is an increasing demand on craftsmen and, moreover, in the developing organization of the established church, the simple lay overseer of the early Christian communities is replaced by the professional priest. At the same time the liturgy gradually evolves into elaborate performances, representing a larger quantity of play, yet requiring at the same time more and more proficient and professional musicians. In sports, the evolution from friendly games on the village green to gigantic mass-entertainments in stadiums, entails builders, coaches, managers, reporters, advertising, transportation, to mention only a few requirements. Similarly one can observe that the increase of aids and technical

methods in education which demonstrates a larger quantity of play in
this field, is commensurate with an expanding amount of labor implicit
in the manufacturing of those aids, the professionalizing of teachers,
and the growing army of administrative personnel.

This, however, relates exclusively to the QUANTITY of proportionate
labor and play. Although it demonstrates to what extent they are
interlocked in the unfolding culture, it is more important, at least for
this examination, to look at the relationship between labor and play
when in the last centuries a change of QUALITY occurs. The question
seems to be what happens to the factor of play itself, and how does its
qualitative change affect the factor of work.

When in coming chapters therefore, we will be scrutinizing the
process of alienation in nineteenth-century culture, we will in fact, without mentioning the terms, concentrate on the changes in the intensity
and in the functioning of the factors of play and labor. Since cultural
alienation, as we have seen in the previous chapter, basically represents
a shift from a subjective to an objective awareness (from spontaneity
to self-consciousness), it must be assumed that this means from the
quality of play to that of labor. Psychologically this can easily be understood. A father and his son playing touch football together, both experience the pleasure of play. But the experiences are of a different
order. The intensity of the son is complete, for he is entirely involved
in the game as such. But in the play of the father extraneous motives
have entered. He plays for the child's sake, for reasons of nostalgia,
because he wants to feel young again, or in an attempt to diminish his
growing paunch. These deliberate intentions do not make the game an
act of labor for him. It is still a game. But the play factor has decreased,
that of labor intruded, and consequently the father's activity, in contrast
to that of his son, has become more mechanical. And although the son's
intensity is greater, the strain on the father is heavier.

Transferring this situation to developments in contemporary civilization, we will find the same gradual change in the nature of our social
institutions and artistic achievements. We have noted above, that the
professionalizing tendency in, for instance, expanding education, brings
with it a greater quantity of labor. But this is only a part of the process.
The spontaneous play-quality itself undergoes changes. The education
which Erasmus receives at the School of the Brethern of Common Life
is infinitely more intense as well as spontaneous than our own well-
planned, endlessly discussed, repeatedly revised methods. It simply
wants to impart as much available knowledge as possible to the student,

for the sake of learning alone. But contemporary education is more and more guided by exterior forces. It has become a service for national or industrial ends, – learning has become almost exclusively a means for obtaining a position. It has lost in intensity and spontaneous excitement, but has gained in practicality. We should not conclude from this that the one kind of education is better than the other. They are merely of a different type. The older one is of an organic creative nature; the contemporary system has, in its deliberate planning and its useful purposes acquired a quality of labor. It goes through the mechanical motions of the teaching of liberal arts; but with decreasing conviction. It is still the game of education. But in giving up a good part of its original autonomy, its play-quality is losing out, it WORKS for outside interests.

The development of a highly sophisticated civilization shows a change from a play-quality to a labor quality, never the reverse. What happens before the flourishing is another matter, not germane to our study. We can only realize the gradual transmutation from a spontaneous, organic order to an administrative, mechanic system. The question whether this change is for the better or the worse is relatively inconsequential, and will not be discussed in this context. It is far more important to recognize it in its essential nature, analyze the underlying historical forces, and describe the manifold varieties in which it reveals itself in our society.

We may, however, conclude from the above that culture is the mutual exchange of dialectically related forces, and define it, not too pedantically I hope, by the formula $c = p \times l$, whereby p represents the factor of play and l that of labor. The further civilizations develop the larger grows the factor l, with the inevitable result of a gradual loss of spontaneity and proportionate increase of mechanization and commercialism.

III

COMMUNICATION AND THE MASSES

> Men will come to be valued more and more, not as
> individuals, but as social functions.
>
> Aldous Huxley

1. THE PRICE OF COMMUNICATION

With the elements of play and labor we have clearly entered the field
of human communication, the very area where social estrangement
reveals itself. Logic requires that we proceed in this direction.

The social existence which we call living together has cultural significance only when it can be recognized as symbolical manifestation, that
is when its configuration carries a clear or hidden historical meaning
within a given era. We are here in the middle of the vast field of communications, which is the inner sense of this living together and which
lies at the roots of the entire problem of what determines cultural history.
There are of course various agencies of conveyance: there are language,
transport, art, music, or love in any degree of physical expression. But
they all make the difference between the individual and society.

Why do we communicate? To answer this is, as we all know, of almost the same order as explaining the concept of man himself. We can
naturally take refuge in such expressions as 'existential loneliness'. But
if we want to elevate this statement above its obvious, sentimental
generality, we are facing the assignment of clarifying the meaning of
man's existentiality, a life's work in itself, and of describing the notion
loneliness as a contrast to accidental loneliness, which is a feasible task
but which by no means solves the problem of human communication.
Leaving then the metaphysical dimension of communication aside, we
can proceed with describing some of its most remarkable characteristics.
We can for instance point to the elements of exchange which link human
beings together and change them from a number of individuals to a
group. Language circulates as a currency. We impart information and

we receive it. The actor needs his audience as much as they need him. Music halls, opera houses and museums would not exist without the basic magnetism of exchange. The touch of a lover's hand confers as much emotional content as it educes. Whatever the essential origin of our social needs, the bridges which we build to the realm of others are exclusively designed for two-way traffic.[1]

The second aspect to notice is the curious play in which the exchange takes place. For that which is transmitted in ordinary or artistic communications is made dubious and often invalidated by a secondary or unconscious intention which symbolically becomes the real object of the communication. Whatever the reason is for the gabble and chatter of teenagers, or for that matter, of adults during coffee-breaks, it far outweighs, although they are not aware of it, the exchange of trivialities in which they are consciously engaged. Gossip information may seem to us of vital importance, but it is only representatively so. Its conveyance stands for an inner social need which far exceeds the significance of the actual narration. Thus it would appear that most if not all of our ordinary language and small talk is symbolic in the sense that its superficial appearance is only a mask of an inner need for association.[2] Clearly this principle underlies the existence of cultivated language and literature as well.[3] Andrew Marvell no doubt must have felt strongly about his 'coy mistress', but for the reader who does not know the maiden and obviously has no interest in getting to know more about her, the possible fascination with the poem about the author and his amatory troubles is awakened by something much deeper than the actual story. This representative play of inner and outer meanings is equally evident outside the confines of language. Naturally in painting a whole new set of esthetic values is involved, yet at the bottom of the creative process that we think painting to be, there is the same mask-situation. The likeness of a Michael Wolgemut which Dürer must convey or that of a Gabriel Emo in a portrait by Tintoretto is the immediate concern of the conscious technique of the artists, but the visitor to art galleries has no interest whatsoever in the men portrayed. The original aim has been

[1] Hegel stresses this element as an exchange (*Tausch*) of negativity and positivity. *Jenenser Realphilosophie*, II, 218.
[2] Harold Goad in *Language in History* (Baltimore, 1958), 11, distinguishes as inward and outward speech the social and psychological functions of language, but does not relate them in a symbolic order.
[3] We are limiting ourselves to the orthodox conception of language, that is as a means of communication only, and leaving aside such hypotheses as those of Sapir and Whorf, who view language also as a molder of thought.

replaced by another, the conveyance of a likeness is substituted by a purpose of a more general nature representing a universal cultural need.

The last characteristic of human communications which is most obviously relevant to our concern, is the estranging effect which appears in all social relationship. In order to establish a bridge with the outer world the subject has to give away a part of its sovereignity to the object; a part of the authenticity of the human self becomes public domain. In this psychological transaction a tiny section of individual self is alienated to the world of 'the others', it is objectivated, that is, it becomes fixed as thing, formula, opinion. It is clearly a natural process, and one which distinguishes man from animal. It is also the source of culture. Animals may form a society, they cannot produce culture. Self-alienation is the price the human consciousness pays for being embedded in a community. It creates its existential unrest, loneliness if one wants, but it also obtains information; it gains the alienation of others. Hegel is the first to analyze it as such. When I have achieved something, I have estranged it from myself; this represents the negative side. But the negative turns into the positive, inasmuch as the estrangement is also an aquisition. "I give nothing away, I alienate nothing, achieve nothing save my word, the language; I want to alienate myself, so does the other ... Precisely therefore do I want to alienate myself, because he, too, wants to alienate himself, and because his negation becomes my position." [4]

As has been noted previously, man's self-estrangement is innate, it belongs to him essentially and existentially. Normally, however, in times which cultural history recognizes as classical periods, the multifarious complexity of life is fastened to a transcendent framework, a principle of life. Man accepts a principle of living which is more or less congruous to his way of living, or at least so he believes. For the twentieth century there is only a way of life, the American way of life preferably, which has no bearing on any pre-formulated principle. In the Middle Ages man's potential social or cultural alienation goes unnoticed because it is laid to rest in the dogma of the Church and for more intellectual minds in scholastic logic. Similarly, the Renaissance man can orientate and fix his restiveness in Cartesian and Newtonian systems. Hegel as the last of the classics finally reviews all the major problems inherent in Western culture and arranges them in a great encyclopedic master-plan for future reference. But after the great wreck-

---

[4] Hegel, *op. cit.*, II, 218.

ing-crew of classical values, with the genius of Kierkegaard, Marx, Strauss, Bakunin, Engels, Stirner or Nietzsche has withdrawn from the field, the framework of principles is shattered and dispersed. For us of the twentieth century there is left this wild freedom, as of a child forever abandoned in a toy department, overwhelmed by the infinite opportunities, but homeless. For us the time-honored categories have become irrelevant and unreliable. Time and place are declared to be only relative, moral is what expedient, we have no truth, except an endless number of truths, no freedom, except any convenient number of freedoms, perspective is dropped from our esthetics, drama has become epic, the tonality of our musical conception is dissolved into serialism, even in science change has replaced causality. So we float. Sometimes we feel as carefree as a cloud on a sunny day. But sometimes we are nostalgic for the solid ground.

It is under such circumstances that man's inherent alienation is activated to such an extent that his sense of community becomes dislodged. He becomes self-conscious about it, he starts to speak about his alienation. He hardly realizes what it means and what it entails. But he has a vague notion that as an individual he is a stranger to the group to which he must belong. In the twentieth century the self-estrangement which is natural and innate in all human communication from a partial transference of the self to the outer world, now comes to be experienced as a total loss of identity in the crowd. Man has become self-conscious about communication itself. Practically all modern philosophies deal with it as an essential problem. Hegel from his early lectures at Jena on recognizes the importance of language as estranging communication,[5] but it is only Kierkegaard who for the first time makes it into a central problem involving the entire human being. Consequently he experiments with the dialectic of the pseudonym to an almost pathological extent. At one point he even gives himself the trouble of attacking his own writings under a *nom-de-plume*, thus sharpening the conflict between subjectivity and objectivity in the problem of communication. Nietzsche sees no other way of conveying his thoughts but in prophetic prose, rhapsodic frenzies or even invectives – an extraordinary replacement of traditional philosophical discourse. In the twentieth century the philosophical concern about communication has become general. The neo-Kantian Ernst Cassirer investigates it as 'symbolic form'. The broad group of philosophical analysts all consider language as the medium by which they conduct their various inquiries, to the extent that it is fair

[5]   *Ibid.*, I, 205, 235 f., II, 212, 218 ff.

to say that philosophical analysis for them is linguistic analysis.[6] Jaspers in his *Philosophie* devotes a large section to existential communication which is one of the revealing clues of all existentialist thinking.[7] Heidegger's consistent method rejects traditional logical demonstration for etymological analysis and does not shy away from poetic communication (Rilke, Hölderlin) in order to discover ontological truths.

The concern about linguistic expression is of course not the only signal of communicative estrangement. But the immediacy of language and its extension into literature makes it naturally one of the most rewarding fields of cultural interpretations. We have already dealt elsewhere in detail with the importance of the factors of work and of play insofar as they are fundamental to the formation of civilization and bear on the emergence of social and individual alienation. To this could be added the increasing role of transportation in the changing awareness of modern society, and in the vast and vague field of love, friendship and family life there are also clear-cut patterns pointing to the historical uniqueness of modern cultural expressions.

2. INDIVIDUAL AND COLLECTIVE

So much scorn has been heaped upon the masses in history that we are defiantly inclined to sing their praise for a change, especially if by doing so we could better accommodate ourselves to the crowds. We can not. For the point is not in the first place whether or not we like, or even tolerate them; one of the remarkable facts of our age is that we are mass-conscious as such. Whence, we may ask, the curious sensitivity about this anonymous monstrosity that seems to haunt our cultural consciousness? Who are the masses? If we stop to think of them in concrete terms, we find that the masses are nowhere around us and in no tangible form can plague us. Only a few of us deal with the masses directly, politicians and actors for instance, and they thrive on them. The ironic twist about our mass-consciousness is that it occurs in the most plebeian of all times when one would expect the fear of the masses to vanish out of history.

The masses have been abhorred ever since Theognis and Plato denounced them. We are not surprised when we find the aristocratic mind of the Renaissance man, whose paragon is the brilliant independent

[6]   J. F. Mora, *Philosophy Today* (New York, 1960), 51.
[7]   Jaspers, *Philosophie*, II, 24-118.

individual, despise the vulgar people. Erasmus's comic hero Folly has a grand time among the ignorant and gullible *vulgus* whom he calls 'that gigantic and powerful monster'.[8] And Petrarch, deploring gluttony and laziness which have banished beauty and wisdom from the world, blames the multitude for its low ambitions:

> "Go needy and naked, o philosophy"
> Thus say the masses, eager for paltry gain.[9]

These are clearly individual expressions which scarcely touch on the social problem of mass power or possible ochlocracy. For that we must move to the times when the crowd becomes a vital political power, an event coinciding with new ideas such as Herder's *Volksgeist*, Rousseau's general will, the common man of Wordsworthian lyrics and Jacksonian America. It is then that thoughtful minds start to wonder what the equalitarian principle, so badly needed and so timely set in motion, may entail in its relentless evolution. We are not of course speaking of the conservative feudalist who desires to maintain a hierarchic order at all cost. The question is not in the first place whether the democratic revolutions at the end of the eighteenth century are beneficial or detrimental in one respect or another, but, granted that they occur by NECESSITY what are their social and cultural ramifications as far as the future is concerned?

The first to be alarmed about the emergence of the multitude is by no means a conservative, but an honorary citizen of the young revolutionary French Republic. Schiller, however, by 1792 begins to relate political convictions to moral and cultural necessities, and from there predicts in 1794, (although he has not heard of Bonaparte yet) that the role of the masses in the developing French Revolution will sooner or later produce dictatorship.[10] In a letter to his friend Körner he expresses his disillusion over the fact that the struggle for just political rights has only brought to light the impotence and lack of dignity in the people and "has thrown back an entire century into barbarism and slavery".[11] To restore mankind to its dignity it needs the education which Schiller proposes in his *Esthetic Letters*, a training in harmony and balance

---

[8]   Erasmus, *In Praise of Folly*, ii, 26.
[9]   "Povera e nuda vai, Filosofia,"
           dice la turba al vil guadagno intesa.
[10] H. C. Mettin, *Der politische Schiller* (Berlin, 1927), 23.
[11] Dated July 13th, 1793. Jonas, III, 333.

which will eventually lead to the establishment of the 'Esthetic State', whose constitutional principle is "to give freedom through freedom".[12]

There is no need to stress the naiveté of this utopian vision. The importance of Schiller's worry lies in the awareness that in the awakening of the populace, a necessary historical achievement, there is an inherent threat to the very liberty it justly struggles to obtain. Schiller recognizes the paradox and concerns himself about an idealistic solution. Goethe does not even try. His harmonious mind distrusts upheavals of any kind, and he admits himself to Eckermann to be no friend of the revolutionary mob "which is bent on robbery, murder and arson, and behind the hypocritical shield of the common good has merely the basest egoistic objectives in mind".[13] Already in the *Venetian Epigrams* of 1790 Goethe warns that the popular uprisings will not only destroy the élite, but also the populace itself:

> Great men went to their downfall; but who protected
> > the rabble
> Against the rabble? Then was the crowd to itself a tyrant.[14]

The ivory-tower outlook of Goethe may not be very helpful in an attempt to understand the real historical problem, but it does focus on the core of the conflict. The idea of a built-in despotism in the emancipation of the lower classes is most remarkably evident in the development of Marxism, which as many political critics have observed shows already from the beginning a rather Prussian mentality. Marx's own autocratic attitude towards contemporary social reformers and rival democratic theories is a signal proof that the trinity of *liberté, egalité, fraternité* has been dethroned. Unlike Fourier and Owen who are driven by compassion and personal experience with working-class misery, Marx's concern with the proletariat is an intellectual one. He stays away from the crowd and despises it. We can understand Engel's letter of February 9, 1851 in which he writes to Marx: "The democratic, the

---

12   *Schiller's Werke*, II, 113.
13   April 27, 1825, *Gespräche*, 437.
14   Grosse gingen zugrunde; doch wer beschütze die Menge
             Gegen die Menge? Da war Menge der Menge Tyrann.
                                          Ven. Epig. 53.
See Ernst Jünger: "Der Demos ist sein eigener Tyrann", *Blätter und Steine*, 221. Is it, one wonders, this rapport between masses and dictatorship that made the people of Moscow, according to a report from the Soviet Union in the *New York Times* of December 7th, 1964, weep at the dying of Stalin, the tyrant, and remain indifferent to the dismissal of Khrushchev, who relieved the tyranny?

red, even the communistic mob will never love us." [15] For them society is not a matter of love, but organization.

The truth of this is most vividly realized by Kierkegaard who stakes his whole life and work on the sovereignity of individual autonomy. We must be careful to distinguish two different though related aspects of the problem. There is the class-struggle of the workers which is an economico-political occurrence, and there is the development of a mass-society involving cultural change. The working-class is a fairly distinct unit which can be described in terms of statistical precision and which can also be treated as having an individual and developing consciousness, as is done, to give an example by Matthew Arnold.[16] But what is a multitude? We rarely meet crowds, and if we do, in sport stadiums at party rallies, we are not aware of them, absorbed as we are in the athletic or political bravura. When we do think of the multitude, it comes to us in an *idée-fixe*, as a haunting bugbear or as a convenient slogan. The masses have no shape in our conception, no identity, no viable character, no beginning or end, no origin or destiny, no location or duration, no rhythm or proportion, no name or property, no extension or direction, no law or fulfillment, no causality or historicity. The masses are a neurosis. The idea of the proletariat in Marxian usage is ambiguous in this respect. When Marx expounds his theories on the economic and political situations of the working class his methods are clearly empirical, and on this basis dialectic materialism can claim to be a scientific system. But proletariat in Marx's thought not only means a group of laborers with particular skills, wages, families and human dignity, it is also a principle of primitive force to be readied for the seizure of the political and industrial machine of the state. This proletarian multitude has no identity at all. It is not worshipped for its virtues as Croce thinks,[17] but rather as an absolute principle. The masses do not make revolution. As history has proved time and again, uprisings are prepared, timed and executed by intellectuals using the brutal bulk-power of the crowds for their own particular ends with the same organizing skills with which absolute monarchs exploit the masses for their primitive wars. The Russian Revolution is no exception. As a doctrine of the proletariat Marxism is greatly confusing in that the

---

[15] Quoted in Leonard Schwarzschild, *Der rote Preusse* (Stuttgart, 1954), 251.
[16] M. Arnold, *Culture and Anarchy*, 90, thinks the working-class (in 1869) "still an embryo, of which no one can yet quite foresee the final development". It has not the experience and self-knowledge of the upperclasses, nor yet its culture, but it has honesty.
[17] B. Croce, *Culture e vita morale: intermezzi polemici* (Bari, 1914), 174.

undeniable scientific foundation of social and economic premises is left when it comes to political aspirations. The Marx of *Das Kapital* is a masterful technician who contributes immeasurably to the solving of broad sociological problems of nineteenth-century industrialism. But as the co-author of the *Communist Manifesto* he loses the scientific demonstration in the slogans of a Utopian Wonderland. As Croce views it, there is a Marx *economista e filosofo* and a Marx *agitatore* "who is the real Marx of Socialism".[18] It is this ambiguity which makes the debate about the question whether Marx ought to be considered as an empirical realist or a theoretical Utopian rather fruitless. He is both.

To go back to Kierkegaard, the only common denominator which he shares with Marx is the rebellious attitude towards Hegel's systematic abstraction of the world as experience into a structure of ideas. Life as a daily realization of possibilities can according to Kierkegaard be understood only in the immediacy of man's individual existence. Therefore any scientific method is objectionable inasmuch as it wants to analyze and describe life. Scientific formulas can never catch the fullness and real essence of man's profound inner needs. In this Kierkegaard thus greatly differs from Marx's empirical analysis of society. To Kierkegaard scientists are the Sophists of modern times and it requires a new Socrates to unmask them.[19] Consequently, the same distrust of the Sophists keeps him away from political considerations. Man cannot be helped by external manoeuvers, he must convert himself inside. There is no room here for ambiguity about the role of the masses. The masses are the arch-enemy of individuality, of the dignity of humanity. They represent the corruption of man's authentic claim: to be himself. The trend of equality finds the most logical fulfillment in levelling.[20]

We are here clearly at a historic juncture. The crucial question between Kierkegaard and Marx is whether the estrangement of man from society must be cured by the restoration of inner personal integrity or by the building up of collective mass-power. The conflict appears under various headings which stand for what many may believe reconcilable forces, but here in their abstract gala-dress represent mutually exclusive worlds: culture or industrialization, religion or science, élite or equalization, individual or evolution.[21] To Kierkegaard man must be saved

18 "La morte del Socialismo", *Ibid.*, 172.
19 Kierkegaard, *Journals*, 181, 184.
20 See III, I, note 57.
21 Denis de Rougemont, *Penser avec les mains* (Paris, 1936), II, 11: "Evolution

from man by cultivating his most distinctive and intrinsic potentialities. He must in the first place be deeply aware of himself, that is see the discrepancies between his existential possibility and his actual failure. Marx, on the other hand, lays the stress on the mobilization of the multitude in order to reinstate the liberty of mankind. The basic characteristic of the masses for which they have been despised throughout the ages, their primitive brutal thrust, is now turned into a major virtue and instrument by which to secure the salvation of the world. Hegel still tries to reconcile the freedom of the community with the freedom of the individual. But after him the components fall asunder. The history of the nineteenth and twentieth century is fundamentally about the separation of the vision of the single from the organization of the many. Kierkegaard and Marx stand at its source. And it is understandable that when at present the ramifications of their initial efforts are manifest in established influential patterns, Communist Marxism shows itself violently hostile to the entire complex of Existential thought.[22] Compromising minds may dream up a conciliatory realm where the two contradicting principles are nibbled down to compatible shapes, (as for instance in Sartre's eclecticism which combines both, together with other disparate ingredients), but the divergence is widening.

Was this estrangement of individual consciousness from the ever-expanding collective consciousness, human responsibility from public opinion, inevitable? Such questions cannot be answered without a number of auxiliary 'ifs' and 'buts' which render the whole historical picture speculatively fuzzy. Perhaps if the surge of the Industrial Revolution had been controlled with more human dignity, if the French Revolution had not burst out of hand to necessitate Napoleonic despotism, if the Romantic movement had not evolved into the later sentimentalism, self-pity or chauvinism, perhaps then the hostility between modern man and his mechanized environment might not have occurred. Who knows? With the data we have at our disposal now, we can only with Burckhardt point to the historic truth that the nineteenth century

---

contre Personne. Nous retrouvons ici le conflit de Marx et de Nietzsche. Mais derrière eux et devant eux, deux noms: Hegel et Kierkegaard dominent et résument ce débat."

[22] The relationship of modern Existentialism and Marxism deserves a better treatment than Georg Lukács's in *Existentialismus oder Marxismus?* (Berlin, 1951). For unfortunately this eminent Marxist scholar here rarely lives up to the erudition and insight of his other works. It is an emotional book which ignores the two most truly Existentialist thinkers, Kierkegaard and Jaspers, entirely, and mainly indulges in invectives on Heidegger and Sartre.

has to develop itself without the old tradition, as a tabula rasa: "I do not extol it, I do not blame it, it is merely a fact." [23] To this he adds apprehensively the question what in the meantime the individual can do in the rootless new era. "The revolution cannot deprive him of one thing: his inner truth." Bruckhardt writes this as a young man who is still not clear about the continuity of his age. But it does not take him long to recognize the true development of the massive conformity which is threatening to asphyxiate the consciousness of the individual. Two years after the statement above, he writes to his friend Kinkel: "There is no talk any longer that man can express himself according to his own motivations. The distress of the time is too great, people cannot develop themselves any longer, they need a common stamp to ensure that every one at all costs may fit into that monstrosity which is called modern life. The few original minds who are able to endure this wretched method without succumbing to it are in their effort to free themselves from inner lies being scorned and scoffed at and then rush to the other extreme." [24] This is a remarkable expression of mid-century premonition, and concern not only about the growing terror of leveling, but also about the inevitable results of extremism of any kind. At the end of his life Burckhardt predicts that the 'rapacity of the masses' will result in despotic authorities.[25]

Burckhardt's *Zeitkritik*, especially towards the end of his life, is not without sour notes intimating a somewhat stick-in-the-mud attitude towards any kind of progress. His work as a whole, however, represents a thoughtful relating of past glories to what he, rightly or wrongly, thinks to be a chaotic disruption of dignity and humanism. Whereas his judgments and forecasts are put forward in the muted tones of chamber-music, with Nietzsche the prophetic warnings acquire a dithyrambic intensity. Unlike both Burckhardt and Kierkegaard he is by no means timid about violence and upheavals, and tries to take the wind out of the Marxist sails by declaring that the will to power, far from being the monopoly of the mob is the legitimate tool to turn people into super-men. Nietzsche's central theme of self-overcoming is an antidotal agency against the increasing mass-organization. Zarathustra imagines himself a strong wind, "the neighbor of the eagles, neighbor of the snow,

[23] Burckhardt, letter to Kinkel, June 13, 1842. In *Briefe Jacob Burckhardts an G. und J. Kinkel* (Basel, 1921), 15.
[24] Written April 26, 1844, but sent to Kinkel as supplement to a letter of July 22, 1846.
[25] Letter to Preen, September 14, 1890. *Jacob Burckhardts Briefe an seinen Freund Friedrich von Preen* (Stuttgart, 1922), 262.

neighbor of the sun", which will blow among the mob and take their breath away.[26] Power is a pure and holy attribute of the solitary élite in the mountains and cannot be shared by the mob, who poison the joy of life with their lascivious dreams.[27] Among Zarathustra's causes for disgust is the modern way of conducting government: "higgling and haggling for power – with the mob". [28] Mob is everything that stands in the way of the fulfillment of Zarathustra's message: impurity, greed, wizened fruit, poisoned wells, stinking fires, and 'maggots in the bread of life".[29]

After such fervent tirades against the riffraff one is tempted to let someone speak up for the masses as a counterpoise to the clarions of the select. One would like to call in a Victor Hugo or a Carl Sandburg to hear them ask indignantly: Who are the people?

> When have the people been half as rotten
> as what the panderers to the people
> dangle before the crowds? [30]

But that would be missing the point. The question which concerns us here is not in the first place how inimical popular opinion, taste and power is to the maintenance of a creative culture, but that the masses in the eyes of leading nineteenth-century thinkers turn their hard-won freedom into a new despotism. To Nietzsche thus the ultimate end of the Socialist movement means the radical 'tyranny of the most insignificant and ignorant'.[31] The feudal and capitalist oppression is being transmuted into a terror of the multitude.

We may, of course, and we do from time to time, challenge each other with the question what the 'people', the 'masses' really represent, in order to lull ourselves into the belief that they actually do not exist at all in the absence of a clearly pin-pointed definition. But this does not deter others of more determined zeal from attempting a detailed psychological description of the masses. Gustave Le Bon, in his *Psychologie des Foules* of 1895 analyzes the decisive role which the masses play in the decline and fall of civilizations. Culture to him can only be led and maintained by a small élite who by the strength of their in-

---

[26]   "Zarathustra", *Werke* (Leipzig, 1896), VI, 143.
[27]   *Ibid.*, 140.
[28]   *Ibid.*, 141.
[29]   *Ibid.*
[30]   Carl Sandburg, *Complete Poems* (New York, 1950), 461.
[31]   *Wille zur Macht*, Aph. 125.

dividuality convey and radiate their refinement to the environment as a whole. The disintegration of culture, on the contrary, is effectuated by the "irresponsible and brutal multitudes rightly qualified as barbarous".[32]

It would be fitting, I believe, to terminate this survey of nineteenth-century vilification of popular power with the judgment of an American author who during a great part of his life reflects with inner concern on the relationship between the individual and the development of a popular movement. The American scene is plainly of utmost importance for the increasing influence of the common man, and no one is more aware of the narrowing scope of the individual than Emerson. His liberal mind sees clearly the necessities for the development of a modern society, but his ardent belief in self-reliance seems in conflict with the new social demands. The inner debate about 'society and solitude' lies at the bottom of his writings as a whole, and remains inconclusive. "To the distress of his friends – those who developed Transcendental premises into an extreme anarchy of individualism, or those who proceeded from the same assumption toward socialism or authoritarianism – Emerson guarded his 'armed neutrality'." [33] Unlike a Thoreau who flees society and despises the mob, Emerson throughout his life is willing and even anxious to negotiate about community and individualism. That his preference lies with the latter is scarcely surprising for a Transcendentalist, but his argumentation is mild and mannered compared with the invectives of a Nietzsche. He pleads for an aristocracy of the mind which is not marked by wealth but by independence. For self-reliance "is the patent of royal nature".[34] He urges his fellow Americans to give up the hope of approbation from the people in the street, if they want to purpose lofty goals.[35] "We have a rich men's aristocracy, plenty of bribes for those who like them; but a grand style of culture, which, without injury, an ardent youth can propose to himself as a Pharos through long dark years, does not exist, and there is no substitute." [36] It is this aristocratic conception of culture which brings Emerson in conflict with the equalitarian tide of the American way of life, for "the true aristocrat is he who is at the head of his own order",[37] and this implies an élite.

[32]   G. le Bon, op. cit., 5.
[33]   The American Transcendentalists, Perry Miller, ed. (New York, 1957), 287.
[34]   Emerson, "Aristocracy", Complete Works, Riverside ed., X, 62.
[35]   Ibid.
[36]   Ibid., 61.
[37]   Ibid., 59.

Emerson's problem is the historical problem of the United States. The conquest of American space and the control of its abundance was achieved by boundless competitive individualism, yet the equalitarian principle which is part and parcel of the new world thus created, proves more and more the leveling force whereby the uniqueness and independence of the pioneer spirit is turned into a grey uniform average. It is this dualism in the American tradition that confuses Matthew Arnold when he discusses its cultural aspects. Appalled by the inequality of his own country, he admires the classless freedom of the American community.[38] He is quick to note, however, that for this very reason the American civilization lacks interest and distinction. While England is becoming more democratic, "the malady here may no longer be that we have an upper class materialized, a middle class vulgarized, and a lower class brutalized. But the predominance of the common and ignoble, born of the predominance of the average man, is a malady too." [39] More than half a century before Matthew Arnold's remark Alexis de Tocqueville with the same liberal yet critical mind views with apprehension the discrepancy between liberty and mass-appeal. His admiration for the American democracy does not prevent him from seeing the dangers and the 'fâcheux effets' of an increasing despotism of the majority.[40] Already then the separation of personal and social freedom is for the astute observer at least painfully evident. The alienating factor in the buoyant society of this new nation is actually at the bottom of the Transcendentalists' Zeitkritik, and to return to Emerson, his eloquent formulations point with precision to the inherent dilemma of the American way of life. "But the people are to be taken in very smal doses. If solitude is proud, so is society vulgar. In society high advantages are set down to the individual as disqualifications. We sink as easily as we rise, through sympathy. So many men whom I know are degraded by their sympathies; their native aims being high enough, but their relation all too tender to the gross people about them. Men cannot afford to live together on their merits, and they adjust themselves by their demerits – by their love of gossip, or by sheer tolerance and animal good nature. They untune and dissipate the brave aspirant." [41]

---

[38] M. Arnold, "Civilization in the United States", *Five Uncollected Essays* (Liverpool, 1953), 51.
[39] *Ibid.*, 64.
[40] Tocqueville, *De la démocratie en Amérique* (Paris, 13me éd., 1850), I, 310.
[41] *Ibid.*, 20.

This a century later, sounds very contemporary to our own ears; the description fits the weaknesses of our own social relations. On the other hand, there is a groping towards an understanding of the equal rights of individual and society which we have long since abandoned. Granted that society we must have, Emerson concludes, it ought to be established on inner relationships. "Society exists by chemical affinity, and not otherwise." Unlike Nietzsche and Kierkegaard, he wants to avoid extreme positions and "keep the diagonal line". "Solitude is impractical, and society fatal. We must keep our head in the one and our hands in the other." [42] If the admonishment does not seem very persuasive in view of the inexorable industrial mobilization of our age, its historic importance lies in the attempt itself to make the American mind aware of the creeping fissure underneath the surface of a blithely and blindly optimistic society. As one of the remarkable prophetic figures who characterize the nineteenth century Emerson, had he lived to see individuality and self-reliance suffocated in the conformity of our century, might have said with Isaiah, "I have labored in vain, I have spent my strength for nought." [43] But that would be overlooking the fact that we, though having lost much of our self-confidence, have gained in awareness of our existential situation.

[42] *Op. cit.*, VII, 20.
[43] *Isaiah*, 49:4.

SURVEY OF NINETEENTH-CENTURY THOUGHT
ABOUT CULTURAL ESTRANGEMENT

> Society everywhere is in conspiracy against the manhood
> of every one of its members.
>
> Emerson

1. BEGINNINGS: SCHILLER, FICHTE, SCHELLING

The nineteenth century is the age of consciousness. It is the age of
history. And because it is an age of awareness of culture, it thinks about
play and about labor. If this century is lacking in passion, as both
Emerson and Kierkegaard complain, it abounds in reflection. Thus it
finds out about man's limitations. From the Renaissance through the
eighteenth century his story has been one of opportunity. Kant's critical
doctrine points to the dawning of a new era. The subjectivity of man
becomes an isolated problem. The isolation of man itself becomes a
problem. The fact of man's estrangement is to determine the thinking
of the nineteenth century.

Hegel is the great name here. As in so many other respects, however,
he merely works out the problems delineated by immediate predecessors. Hegel does not succeed Kant, as is suggested in many hasty pres-
entations of intellectual history. His work is rooted in the post-Kantian
polarities of Fichte, Schiller and Schelling.

The town of Jena for a short period takes up the center of the stage.
It becomes the nursing ground for one of the most decisive ways of
thinking in modern times: dialectic logic. Not unrelatedly, it produces
the first thoughts on alienation. Moreover the town becomes the birth-
place of the Romantic movement. The university at Jena has been a
rather sleepy place until the new Kantian doctrine invades its premises.
Then it starts to appoint eminent scholars such as Griesbach, Reinhold,
Paulus. From 1789 on, during no more than fifteen years, it attracts
to its faculty the names of Schiller, Fichte, Schelling, and Hegel, thereby
gaining a world reputation. The new academic thinking is closely inter-

woven with the literary movement. Hegel is a friend of Hölderlin's. Fichte and Schelling represent the philosophical doctrines of the Romanticists, Schiller's work has a profound influence on that of Hölderlin, and his theories generate the new ideas launched in 1798 by the Schlegels in the *Athenäum*.[1]

Schiller has been called the 'father' of alienation, an epithet as romantic as it is inaccurate. For such notions of general concern are rarely sired by a specific mind; rather they emerge from a latent state of collective consciousness. Yet, though the idea of alienation is a communal product of the last decade of the eighteenth century, Schiller must be credited with first formulating it in an unequivocal manner, thereby starting a historical development which runs through Hegel's work to the Communist Manifesto. The passage most frequently quoted occurs in the sixth letter of the *Esthetic Education* (1795): "Enjoyment has been separated from labor, means from ends, effort from reward. Man, forever tied to a particular small fragment of the whole, cultivates himself only as a fragment; with the continuous, monotonous noise in his ears of the wheel which he turns, he can never develop his mind harmoniously, and instead of expressing the natural essence of mankind, he becomes merely a copy of his work or his knowledge."[2]

A remarkable aspect of this passage is the emphasis on the economico-social conditions of the time, for which Schiller rarely shows as much concern as for the political, moral and esthetic problems. It is in every respect a classical statement on the dehumanization process which, under the increasing impact of the Industrial Revolution, becomes the most formidable threat to the humanist tradition in Europe. Since the element of alienated labor seems to be the key issue in this passage, it is understandable that social and political theorists have given it so much attention. Some have seen it as a document, pointing far beyond its own age, and to be fully understood only in ours.[3] This is undoubtedly true. But the expressiveness of Schiller's statement should not distract us from the fact that it represents only a part of his concern about the dehumanization of man. The entire series of twenty-seven letters deals with this problem and within the sixth letter itself the range is far wider

---

[1]   See Arthur O. Lovejoy, "Schiller and the Genesis of German Romanticism", *Essays in the History of Ideas* (New York, 1960), 207-228.
[2]   Schiller, *Werke*, XI, 17.
[3]   Franz Neumann, *The Democratic and the Authoritarian State* (Glencoe, Ill., 1957), 272.

than the sociological treatment of labor. Its appeal is directly to the totality of society.

The description of the limitations of the age is set against the background of the Greek golden age, which to Schiller represents the fullest human harmony. In contrast, he believes his own age to be suffering from too much analytic intellect which has created disorder in the arts and sciences. To make the dehumanization complete the national governments have become complicated clockworks, operating with an infinite number of mechanical parts. Thus individual 'concrete life' is sacrificed for an abstract machinery, "and the state remains for ever alien to its citizens".[4] Schiller admits that this mechanical way of life, detrimental though it be for the individual, is the only means to advance the collective (*Gattung*).[5] His main argument rests on the evil of one-sidedness with which the modern age encourages specialists. Thus, he maintains, metaphorically, we will be able to develop muscled athletes, but a beautiful body demands a free play of all its parts.[6]

The key notions in this letter are separation, disorganization, harmony, and totality. They recur in numerous variations throughout the entire work. The basic constituent elements of the harmonious man, his natural instincts and his formative intellect, become separated and only a new consciousness of totality will save him. This split in man's mind is reflected in society as a whole: on the one hand, there is among the masses a lawless desire for power and violence, while on the other the educated classes indulge in luxury, a fact "the more disturbing because civilization itself is its source".[7]

The theme of the harmonious integration of the individual in society runs as a persistent motif through all Schiller's writings. The idea of man's dignity, again, is an expression of inner balance, of the totally integrated mind which alone can guarantee a free humanity. It occurs in his easy *On Grace and Dignity*, and it is already visible in his first play *Die Räuber*. His poetry repeatedly shows a yearning for the integration of man with nature, as it was in ancient times (*Die Götter Griechenlands*) and as it may be once again.[8] In his letters to the Prince

---

[4]   Schiller, *op. cit.*, XI, 19.

[5]   *Ibid.*, 20.

[6]   *Ibid.*, 22.

[7]   Fifth letter, *ibid.*, 13. Schiller in all likelihood is here influenced by Adam Ferguson who in his *Essay on the History of Civil Society* criticized the age for its luxury and warned against disasters resulting from its boasted refinements and sophistication (Dublin, 1776), 346.

[8]   "Der Spaziergang", *Werke*, XVII, 23.

of Augustenburg, which constitute the preparation for the *Esthetic Letters*, his attacks on the depravity of modern society are unrestrained. On July 13th, 1793 he writes: "A polished and consistent Epicureanism has begun to stifle the energy of character and, the chains of need tightening more and more, the increased human dependence on things physical has gradually led to the point where the principles of passivity and docile obedience represent the highest standard of life. Hence the limitation in thought, the impotence of action, the miserable mediocrity of production which to its shame characterize our age." [9]

Schiller's thorough analysis of the age, through the depth of his intuition, is far ahead of his time and fully proves its basic correctness only in the twentieth century. Without much concrete knowledge of the Industrial Revolution, which has not even begun in his own country, and without detailed data of the political revolutions still developing at that time (1795), he probes the essential problems of that period with devastating detachment. This is the more remarkable since, unlike Edmund Burke, he is a liberal ardently committed to fight the suppression of human rights. And according to his reasoning it is precisely for the furthering of human rights that he projects his education for the new 'esthetic' man.

One can hardly blame Schiller for not knowing more about the details and the economic, social, and political ramifications of the contemporary problems which might have qualified his statements. A more founded criticism could be, and has been, directed against his unwarranted comparisons with the Greek civilization, of which he has only a vague and inadequate conception. The alleged harmonious nature of Hellas is a Greek ideal suggested to us by works of sculpture, architecture and literature, but the assumption that therefore the Greek citizen of say, Pericles' time is more totally man than Schiller's contemporary, cannot be substantiated. To be sure, the play-element, the AGONAL character which means so much to Schiller for a balanced culture, is clearly strong in Athens at the height of its history and, as he demonstrates convincingly, badly on the wane in the eighteenth century. But he never distinguishes different periods in the history of Greece, which renders the comparison with his own age rather invalid.

Schiller suffers from the Romantic habit of dreaming of a Golden Age of the past, which must be restored in the future. Clearly the historical situation in Greece is so unlike that of eighteenth-century

[9] Jonas, III, 334.

Europe that, if a restoration is called for at all, it can scarcely be constructed on the framework of an ancient society. The dream of a lost Arcadia, which he elsewhere expresses in poetic terms,[10] is indicative for the spirit of the time itself.[11] The feelings of being a stranger in one's own time coincide with the first gropings around the phenomenon of alienation. Obviously on this basis one cannot come to grips with the very concrete deficiencies which one may detect in contemporary society. Accordingly, Schiller's proposed remedy of overcoming dehumanization by restoring man's integrity of character is a noble, but meaningless gesture in view of the remorseless mechanization and industrialization which at that time are about to change the structure of man's life.

The importance of Schiller's analysis lies chiefly in the clear vision of man's threatened position in an entirely new social order. What others only vaguely sense, he is able to formulate in strong, vivid wording. Relying too much on his intuitive insights, his treatment of details is often fuzzy or inaccurate, while the logic of his speculations is sometimes deficient. Nevertheless, the *Esthetic Letters* represent a classical document in that they for the first time present the great problems concerning alienation and dehumanization which are to occupy the nineteenth century. They prepare the way for a new thinking on state and citizen, need and satisfaction, as it is to be elaborated in the writings of Hegel and Marx.[12] They are equally important as the first *Zeitkritik* of a long series to come. The consciousness of an own age is already evident in Herder's letters on Humanity (1792), in which he asks: What is the spirit of the age? (*Zeitgeist*). His answer: it is the sum of the thoughts, moods, impulses and vital forces which express themselves in a historical process.[13] It is foremost the servant of humanity. And it is for the integrity and totality of humanity that Schiller, like Herder, makes his case.

But unlike Herder, he sees clearly that the realization of this ideal is thwarted by the increasing estrangement of the individual from his natural roots. The solution he offers is a dialectic idealism: originally

[10] "Auch ich war in Arkadien geboren" (1783), *Werke*, III, 4.
[11] For the widespread interest in this theme, see Erwin Panofsky, "Et in Arcadia ego", *Philosophy and History*, R. Klibansky and H. J. Paton, editors (New York, 1963), 223-255.
[12] H. Popitz, *op. cit.*, 29, 31. To what extent Hegel was directly influenced by Schiller is difficult to assess. He did admire the *Esthetic Education*. In a letter to Schelling of April 16, 1795, he declares it to be 'a masterpiece'.
[13] Herder, *Briefe zur Förderung der Humanität* (Augsburg, 1946), 43, 44.

integrated in nature, man, through the corruption of high civilization, is alienated from this realm and can only be brought back to a state of harmony in a third phase, that of 'Great Nature' which is not barbaric nature, but a synthesis of man's acquired intellect and his sensate faculties, balanced out in a playful freedom.

Less influential and with less sense of historical urgency are the contributions of both Fichte and Schelling to the understanding of alienation. Yet they confirm once more how much the new awareness is part of a collective awakening to man's changed reality. It is linked up with the preoccupation with the 'spirit of the age' started by Herder and analyzed further in Fichte's *Die Grundzüge des gegenwärtigen Zeitalters*, originally lectures given at Berlin in 1805 and 1806, Novalis's *An die Christenheit* and Arndt's *Geist der Zeit*. One can hardly think of a more nebulous and potentially dangerous concept with which to operate, but for the Romanticist's mind this is more an attraction than a burden. Schelling, a Romanticist at heart, as a trained thinker attempts all his life to harness and formalize mysterious conceptions. Starting out with a philosophy of nature, he ends up late in life as a proto-Existentialist with what he calls a 'positive philosophy'. Fichte, first making his reputation with a highly subjectivistic idealism, ends his life at the center of a new nationalistic Germany: the university of Berlin, whose first rector he becomes. Both Fichte and Schelling know Schiller at Jena, but there are no indications of a particularly friendly rapport between them. On the contrary, the relationship between Fichte and Schiller is soon disturbed by an unpleasant exchange of letters. Yet, though the personalities do not blend, their professional contact is highly important for the intellectual history of the time. Their common concern focuses on such newly emerged problems as polarity, the mutual exchange in polarity (Fichte's *Wechselwirkung*), and the triad dialectic of thesis-antithesis-synthesis.

Fichte's concern with alienation is mainly theoretical. It is he who for the first time uses the term in the modern sense. Originally it is a legal expression connected with the transference of ownership of goods. Grotius uses it in this sense,[14] and so does Rousseau,[15] except that they follow the Romans in including the 'goods' of man's liberty, which are alienated in the case of slavery. Fichte in his *Wissenschaftslehre* of 1794, applies it metaphysically, as part of an absolute totality being posited

---

[14]   Grotius, *De iure belli ac pacis*, III, x, 6, III, xx, 5.
[15]   Rousseau, *Contrat social*, I, ii, I, iv, I, vi.

as object. His reasoning is highly intricate, and it would be an impossible assignment to produce an adequate abridgment of the many pages of close thinking which deal with such technical terms as *Setzen* (positing), *Nicht-setzen* (non-positing), *Wechsel* (exchange), or *Wirksamkeit* (activity) which hardly bear translation. All we can attempt is to point to the historical place of this kind of thinking, which concentrates on the relationship of the Self (*Ich*) and the phenomenal world with which it communicates. The self, as total subjectivity, must deal with the concrete facts of the world, and it does so in a transaction which represents a polarity (*Wechselwirkung*) between the subject and the objective world. In this polar relationship a part of the infinite subjectivity of the self is made a specific object, that is, it is ex-pressed (*entäussert*), it is alienated from the self as absolute freedom, it is so to speak ex-cluded from it.[16]

It is significant that almost at the same time (and exactly in the same year as Schiller's *Esthetic Letters*) Schelling arrives at similar conclusions of the objectivation of the self. In his *Vom Ich als Prinzip der Philosophie* he uses the same term exclusion (*Ausschliessung*) to indicate how the self, the I which according to its essence is absolute freedom,[17] excludes the non-I, the outer objectivity from its universality, its absolute domain. [18] This 'pure self' is unconditioned in the sense of unlimited by objects. Thus the utterances of the I, the normal communications of the self in its community, is a conditioning by which, according to Schelling, the infinite freedom of the self is limited in the laws and spatial dimensions of the objects. It is objectivated (*be-Dingt*).[19]

It is not difficult to see, relating these abstract speculations to the general contemporary problems, that behind them stands the polarity of individual and species. Polarity to both Fichte and Schelling is the key to all metaphysical problems, but they are well aware of the fact that it derives from a physical quality. Schelling's academic training includes physics and chemistry and in his early works he likes to indulge in the discussion of scientific phenomena. Thus it is understandable that he comes to the conclusion that all quality is electricity.[20] But behind him and Fichte stands the towering figure of Herder, who in so many respects starts new trends of thinking which are to become of decisive

16   Fichte, *Sämmtliche Werke* (Berlin, 1845), I, 165.
17   Schelling, *Werke* (Leipzig, 1907), I, 31.
18   *Ibid.*, 29.
19   *Ibid.*, 18.
20   *Ibid.*, 707.

importance through the nineteenth into the twentieth century. The concept of magnetism with its moments of attraction and repulsion represents to Herder the basic principle of all life.[21] Its significance is not lost on the scientific mind of Schelling, nor on that of Goethe who already in his essay on Nature of 1790 writes about the polarity of contraction and expansion.[22] The idea of polarity runs through the nineteenth century where it becomes absorbed in Vitalist thinking, in the historical theory of Henry Adams, and later, with special insistence, in the works of Spengler.

Fichte, near the end of his career, gives his lectures on the historical significance of the age. The development of man from primitivism to perfection, according to him goes through five successive stages: the state of innocence, of incipient sin, of total sinfulness, of incipient justification, and of complete justification and sanctification. [23] History is seen from the point of view of religion, rational religion (*Vernunftreligion*), as Fichte calls it, and by this standard his own time falls in the third phase, that of complete sinfulness.[24] The details of this critique do not concern us here, nor the validity of its religious foundation. But it shows the remarkable trend whereby philosophers for the first time since Socrates turn to the evils of their own age, and not surprisingly this coincides with a growing popularity of the Greek thinker.[25] The Enlightenment in general is quite contented with itself, and most of its representative thinkers look down on previous centuries as barbarous times which they have gloriously overcome. Schiller himself, by no means a true exponent of the *Aufklärung*, describes with unrestrained pride in his Inaugural Address of 1789 the differences between earlier times and his own age as a contrast of slavery and liberty.[26] But this unbridled optimism changes within a few years, and the *Esthetic Letters* testify to the result. Even Herder, by no means a disappointed pessimist by nature, describes with apprehension the drift towards lawlessness on the one hand, and the arrogance of the rich on the other as the dangerous extremes of his time.[27]

---

[21] Quoted in Johannes Hoffmeister, *Goethe und der Deutsche Idealismus* (Leipzig, 1932), 33.
[22] See Hoffmeister, *ibid.*, 29, who compares this with Hegel's "the magnet represents in a simple and naive manner the nature of the philosophical concept".
[23] Fichte, "Die Grundzüge des gegenwärtigen Zeitalters", *ibid.*, VII, 11.
[24] *Ibid.*, VII, 18.
[25] Socrates was especially honored in the work of Frans Hemsterhuis who had a considerable influence on Herder, Fichte, Novalis and Goethe.
[26] For an analysis of this address, see the author's *Freedom and Dignity*, II, 2.
[27] Herder, *op. cit..* 46, 47.

Schelling, after having survived Schiller, Fichte and Hegel, at the end of his life delivers at the University of Berlin a *Zeitkritik* of an entirely different nature. It is directed against the growing Hegelian doctrine, and the religious ciritcism prevailing after Hegel's death. Naturally it has a limited academic scope only. Yet since this critique eventually stimulates Existentialist philosophy it remains of historical importance. The development of the notion of Existence as a basis for modern thinking will be discussed elsewhere. As for Schelling's mythological *Weltanschauung* which forms the core of this new 'positive' philosophy, it has little or no impact on this time. The religious attitude has changed. Neither Schelling's mysticism, nor Fichte's *Vernunftreligion* are compatible with the new age. It is the radical criticism of Hegel's followers, Strauss, Feuerbach, Bauer, Marx and Stirner, which is to be of decisive significance for the history of religion, be it in a negative way.

The early phase of the history of alienation thus is closely allied with age-consciousness and age-critique. It ought to be stressed, however, that *Zeitkritik* in itself is not necessarily an expression of cultural estrangement. One may accompany the other merely in the relationship of their social awareness, especially if the questions of individuality, human character, self-reliance, etc., etc., are raised. The thoughts of Schiller, Fichte, and Schelling are reflections of a period characterized by transition. They seem to look backward and forward at the same time: to the past which is irrevocably lost, to the future where mankind can be saved only by a new way of thinking. Especially with Schiller and Fichte this new era is dependent on the education of man towards a new ideal, but underneath nearly all the writings of this period lies a dialectic necessity. The age is supposed to be antithetic to a previous one, but it will be regenerated in a new era of harmonious synthesis.[28]

2.   ESTABLISHMENT: HEGEL, GOETHE, WAGNER

Strictly speaking, there is little specific social critique in Hegel's writings. Starting his career in Jena, he founds jointly with his friend Schelling, the critical *Journal der Philosophie* in which (in 1802) an article appears on philosophical criticism and its relation to the contemporary situation. Towards the end of the discourse Hegel submits that philosophy is fundamentally of an esoteric nature, and ought not

[28]   Popitz, *op. cit.*, 15.

to be popularized. For popularization to him is actually vulgarization.[29] In this he directs himself against a trend greatly favored by the Enlightenment, especially by Voltaire and the Encyclopedists, who are highly succesful in transmuting complicated and technical ideas, for instance those of Newton, into simplified versions. The fallaciousness of popularization, Hegel thinks, lies in the fact that it bases itself on common sense and common intelligence (*Verstand*) which is a 'local and temporal limitation', directly opposed to philosophy.[30] Referring to Aristotle, Hegel believes that the people ought to raise themselves to the level of philosophy. Philosophy should not stoop to accommodate the people. "In these days of freedom and equality, however, in which a large public has been formed that does not want to miss anything . . . the best and most beautiful have not escaped the fate . . . of being manipulated until they are vulgar enough to be appropriated." [31] Thus the levelling of values has been proclaimed to be respectable work. No field of culture is safe from this process. The moment a new idea in art or philosophy appears, it is put in a popular compendium for domestic use. The assumption is made either that anything of a philosophical nature can be made popular, or that anything of a popular content can be transformed into philosophy.[32]

This sounds pretty much like the arrogance of the élite, an attitude hardly tolerable to our egalitarian cast of mind. But we must tolerate the historical phenomena in themselves and their time. Hegel's view clearly concurs with the then prevalent idea (still held by many, incidentally) that history and culture are a product of a small minority, and if one desires to participate in this product in one way or another one simply has to rise to the level of the minority. The idea of an intellectual minority lowering its precepts and standards to bring them within the reach of the masses is sheer decadence to Hegel.

At the bottom of this decline lies the 'spirit of unrest and instability', so characteristic of the age. It is expressed philosophically as well as politically in a dangerous DUALISM,[33] against which man ought to safeguard himself. Why and how Hegel from this situation derives that the sciences have become dead and boring is unclear. The judgment seems, moreover, to go against the historical facts as we know them. The

29 Hegel, *Sämtliche Werke* (Lasson, ed.), I, 126.
30 *Ibid.*, 126.
31 *Ibid.*, 127.
32 *Ibid.*, 127-128.
33 *Ibid.*, 128.

schism itself, of course, is verifiable enough, and whether for better or worse, the separation of Reason (*Vernunft*) and intelligence (*Verstand*) as Hegel assesses it is an equally undeniable factor. We can long debate about the question – a crucial one – whether this historical split wrecks the intellectual disciplines and cultural expressions. Hegel believes this to be so, and here singles out the sciences and religion. The most important point, however, is the consciousness of a situation which Hegel in this section describes as an estrangement of intelligence from reason, but one which is part of a far more universal trend of cultural estrangement.

The overcoming of this dualism is the one great recurrent theme of all Hegel's major writings. Although he later rarely deals with the decline of the age in this specific manner, his philosophical system in its entirety is a confirmation of his belief that the great historical manifestation of the Western world is finished. The rest will be a story of petering out and withering away. Philosophy now has to analyze in grey tones (abstractions) how the actuality of the past happened. Hegel's self-assigned task is to reconcile the historical dualism of Western civilization in a unity which can exist only in the transcendence of the philosophical Idea. Thus his thoughts constitute a theoretical remedy of alienation, despite the fact that Hegel seldom mentions the word in his later writings.

A polemical battle has been going on among Hegel specialists as to whether or not the *Phänomenologie des Geistes* should be considered as the first part of his total system, or rather as an introductory preparation for the later works to come.[34] It has little relevancy to our concern. As far as the idea of alienation goes, the *Phenomenology* gives all the required answers to see how Hegel's entire panoramic treatment tries to solve the conflict of estrangement in an abstract harmony of thought. In the previous chapter this problem has been discussed in the context of labor. In a sense all human actions constitute work inasmuch as they transform physical energy into more or less useful products. In the *Phenomenology* the process of estrangement is viewed as an actualization of the Self, the consciousness. Human actions express this consciousness, and form reality. By thus creating the practical world something of the essence of the Self is lost, or rather is transferred to the

---

[34] See on this Otto Pöggeler, "Zur Deutung der Phänomenologie des Geistes", *Hegel-Studien*, F. Nicolin and O. Pöggeler, editors (Bonn, 1961), 255-295. Hegel originally suggested to Schelling that the work was supposed to be a general introduction to his philosophy. *Briefe*, I, 132, 161.

world of objects. This process is that of the 'self-alienating mind', which Hegel sees as an exteriorization and a release of the essence (*Entwesung*) of the individual itself.[35]

There is nothing debasing or dehumanizing in this situation; on the contrary, it is the most typically human condition, the one whereby man exists, whereby he becomes a social, instead of a self-seeking, self-contained being. In dealing with his social environment, in fulfilling the common needs of life as a human organization, man automatically sacrifices something of his self-being, his individuality. The personality thus alienating itself, gives shape to the practical world to which he relates as a stranger.[36] This shape-giving cultivation (*Bildung*) of the Self in the world of objects and practical realities is the actual validity of the individual, "Inasmuch as it has formation (*Bildung*), it has reality and power." [37] The Self strives towards expression and exteriorization in order to deal with the social exigencies, and it does so by imparting its being to the other world. It becomes real by suspending its own inner authenticity. This process, one of communication, obviously reveals itself most strongly in language. The power of language 'executes' that which is to be brought into the open. It is the representative of the Self, and the agent of the self-limiting (*für-sich-sein*) element of the self-consciousness when this is put into reality, so that it has a purpose for others.[38]

It would appear that the element of alienation described here, according to Hegel, is inherent in man as a social being. Nothing, however, gets really lost in the separation which occurs, for it is reconciled in an abstract process which Hegel's philosophy offers, namely the medium of the philosophical Idea. This highly theoretical construction of how the alienation of the Self is suspended in the synthesis of the pure and absolute Self is difficult to demonstrate other than in a technical detailed discourse, which here would be out of order. For all practical purposes it suffices to understand that any unresolved separation of the I and the non-I (the objective world formed by the I) must result in that which Hegel believes to be a dangerous dualism. There is of course no point here in agreeing or disagreeing with Hegel's philosophical exposition on the basis of intrinsic merits, since we have taken it out of the strictly technical context. Historically speaking, however,

---

[35] Hegel, *op. cit.*, II, 347.
[36] *Ibid.*, 351.
[37] *Ibid.*
[38] *Ibid.*, 262.

it is important to know that that which Hegel means by dualism is the beginning of the very phenomenon we are examining here.

Hegel, while observing the growing rift in the consciousness of individual and world as it reveals itself, among others, in the writings of the Romanticists, (and as he sees it in the life of his friend Hölderlin), directs himself against this pathological yielding to vague nostalgia and unresolved living. At the age of thirty he realizes the need to abandon the dreams and ideals of his youth and turn to the actuality of the world. For only by getting to know and becoming a functional part of society as it operates can the reconciliation between ideal and practice, individual and community, be found. In order to achieve this Hegel turns his youthful probing into a 'system', as a natural result of reflection and academic pursuit.[39] Why the dualism of the age which Hegel deplores should have to be overcome in a system of abstractions, may seem mystifying in our practical world, where instant remedies are advertised for all alleged evils in society. But one must keep in mind that to him the actuality of the historical Western world has been completed, and that the 'system' is a comprehensive presentation of this world in philosophical terms. At this juncture of history, philosophy is esentially encyclopedic, Hegel believes, because its truth can be in TOTALITY alone.[40]

Needless to say that this state of totality can be attained only in an abstract Idea, which Marx calls a mystification, but which Hegel presents as the true reality in a world practically cracking up into disconnected fragments. This deliberate construction of metaphysical harmony is typical for the Idealist philosophy of the time, and reminds one of Schiller's attempt to reconcile the contrasting elementary drives, the sensate and the intellectual, in an 'esthetic' state where absolute freedom will prevail. The revolutions of the eighteenth century, that is the political upheavals, the industrial expansions, and the Romantic movement have torn man's consciousness and only if he can be educated to a new awareness of the 'esthetic' freedom, will the rift be healed. Schiller's notion of the esthetic is fundamentally that which in Hegel's system is meant by totality.

Entirety (*das Ganze*) is also the predominant theme in Goethe's work. That which Hegel develops by logical demonstration, Goethe sees in poetic symbols by the strength of imagination. Much has been written about the remarkable similarities which show up in the major concerns

[39] Hegel to Schelling, Nov. 2, 1800, *Briefe*, I, 59. Cf. Löwith, I, iii, 4.
[40] *Enzyklopädie*, 7.

of these two men. The early Hegel disciples try to illustrate the glory of the master with Goethe's poetry, until F. T. Vischer around 1840 starts a trend to approach Hegel rather from Goethe's work.[41] Eckermann reports that Goethe with the exception of some of the philosopher's ideas thinks highly of Hegel.[42] On October 18, 1827 Goethe invites Hegel to a tea at which the dialectic method is discussed. Hegel, according to Eckermann, regards dialectic as a natural way in which to distinguish the true from the false. Goethe, agreeing with this, adds the warning, however, that dialectic ingenuity can easily be misused to such an extent that the true is made false and the false true. When Hegel retorts that such manipulations are tried only by neurotic (*geistig kranke*) minds, Goethe concludes this part of the conversation with the remark that the study of nature prevents the dialectic principle from being applied in a corrupted sense.

The outstanding principle which both Hegel and Goethe accept as the basic instrument with which to operate is the idea of polarity. Clearly behind them stands the figure of Schelling with his nature philosophy. Thus to Goethe the whole physical experience is expressed in antitheses: [43]

> Two souls,
> Mind and matter,
> God and world,
> Thought and extension
> Ideal and real,
> Sensuality and idea,
> Phantasy and intelligence,
> Being and yearning.
>
> Two sides of the body,
> Right and left,
> Breathing.
> The physical experience:
> The magnet.

But for Goethe as well as Hegel the crowning idea is that which results

[41] H. Falkenheim, *Goethe und Hegel* (Tübingen, 1934), 2. Cf. J. Schubert, *Goethe und Hegel* (Leipzig, 1933), 14.
[42] *Gespräche*, 507.
[43] Goethe, *Naturwissenschaftliche Schriften* (Weimar, 1893), XI, 165.

from polarity, the synthesis of totality. Goethe, often taking exception to Hegelian terms, instead of synthesis prefers *Steigerung* which is the intensification as well as elevation of two contrasting principles resulting in a higher unity. The fusion on a lower level will be merely an indifferent mixture, but *Steigerung* implies a third, new, higher, unexpected entity.[44]

To Goethe the essential truths which nature reveals find their analogues in a metaphysical sense. Man's consciousness registers the polarity of physical phenomena, but his own activity depends on it in equal measure. The quality of his efforts is determined by the intensity of his imagination. That which the magnet represents in nature, is the symbol for the operation of the mind. In a letter of March 18, 1801 Goethe writes to Schiller that artists and writers learn to raise prosaic reality to the level of poetic symbolism, whereby symbols to him mean representatives "which carry within them a certain totality".[45] Totality is the productive, creative, the generative aspect of nature as well as culture; it is the idea of the wholesome that is to mean so much to Nietzsche's philosophy of life. In the *Goetzendämmerung* Nietzsche says of Goethe that he fought the separation of reason and sensuality and that he therefore "disciplined himself to totality".[46]

Nothing disturbs Goethe more than the divisive forces which he sees arise in his age to threaten the poised sovereignity of culture. These disuniting forces are in the political upheavals as well as in the Romantic movement. Although he recognizes the urgency of humanitarian rights for which the French Revolution battles, and the liberation from ossified forms which is the aim of the Romanticists, he will have no part in these crusades if they entail a fissure in the structure of society. The separation of reason and sensuality to which Nietzsche refers, is in Goethe's mind clearly encouraged by the excesses of the time, be they of a political or artistic nature. Goethe offers no theories of alienation; he does not pretend to have Hegel's analytical powers. Relying, however, on his strong intuition, he according to Löwith diagnoses 'the general disease of the age' as an inability "to express (*entäussern*) its subjectivity productively, and to come to grips with the objective world".[47] The very quality of the intuitive judgment does not need specific argumentations, and Goethe consequently does not produce a *Zeitkritik* such as those of

[44]   *Ibid.*, 166. Cf. also 11.
[45]   J. Schubert, *ibid.*, 48.
[46]   Nietzsche, *Werke* (Leipzig, 1899), VIII, 163.
[47]   K. Löwith, *op. cit.*, 17.

Schiller, Fichte or Hegel. Yet in his letters and conversations, especially at the end of his life, when it is clear to him that the revolutionary upheavals continue to upset the balance of civilization, Goethe turns to what he thinks are the evils of the time. The new literary works that come to his attention, he calls a 'literature of despair', with its accents on the ugly, negative, and horrible. Everything is directed towards the 'ultra', and modern man, while over-bidding and over-reaching himself in order to cling to his mediocrity, becomes ever more extreme and vulgar.[48] In this feverish drive for outward effect, every profound study and every gradual and thorough development of natural talent is excluded.[49]

The revolution of 1830 confirms Goethe's doubts about the future of Western civilization. As a too close contemporary he has little understanding of some of the productive undercurrents of the liberal movement, a defect exacerbated by his persistent withdrawal into a spiritual ivory tower. These limitations notwithstanding, Goethe, like Hegel, sees correctly that the ideal of unity and totality is more and more made impossible, and the cultural division widening to an alarming degree. The two worlds, that of the senses and that of the Idea, far from finding their higher unity, oppose each other in an increasingly hostile manner. Goethe's *Faust* is essentially the story of the overcoming of this separation. The Faustian search as the prototype of the Western ideal can be, and has been, dogmatically exaggerated. Yet allowing for the limitations of all type-casting, Faust does represent the symbolic expression of modern man's reconciliation of the two worlds within his breast: [50]

> Two souls are dwelling in my breast,
> which strive to be divided each from each;
> One clings with an impassioned lust
> To the fair world of outer seeming;
> The other rises from the dust
> To heights of visionary dreaming.

This sets the scene for the situation of modern estrangement, which drives Faust to act as he does, in his feverish search, leaving behind him failure after failure. The tragic in Faust is the recognition of Western

---

[48]   Quoted in Löwith, *ibid.*, 44. See for Goethe's and Hegel's attitude towards the revolutionary changes at the beginning of the 19th century, Löwith, 42 ff.
[49]   Eckermann, 550.
[50]   *Faust, I*, Scene with Wagner before the City Gate.

man that, having arrived at the top and cultivated himself to the highest state of knowledge, he yet cannot live in peace with his own world.

Goethe's kinship to Hegel, so patently established in the concentration on the idea of totality, is no less clearly revealed in the belief that an inner idea works toward expression, and that nature, the phenomenal world, is but an actualization of the spirit. For Goethe this is simply a matter of mystical perception, not unlike the way in which Jakob Boehme arrives at his judgment that "the inward always strives toward expression".[51] To Hegel, however, the actualization of the spirit is a reasonable process that one can put in a logical system, as indeed he does in the *Phenomenology*. It is therefore by no means far-fetched to compare this work to Goethe's *Faust*, for the Faustic in the *Phenomenology* and the phenomenological in *Faust* are mutually present.[52] And one of Goethe's 'maxims' confirms that Idea is that which always becomes phenomenon and "thus appears to us as the law of all phenomena".[53]

Goethe comes to this conclusion not only by poetic reflection, but also by thorough scientific studies which occupy a great part of his life. It is therefore important in our own time, when the hostility between the sciences and the humanities in the academic world becomes increasingly marked, to see how Goethe already senses this and stresses the essential need to overcome this cleft. He recognizes the validity of observation and empirical science as the basis for understanding nature, yet accuses the Sensationalist school of having separated the natural phenomena from man. Richarda Huch, in her book on dehumanization, in this connection remarks that Goethe holds against Bacon that his study of the physical world is not conducted *ex analogia hominis*, that is, Bacon treats nature as if it can be divorced from man's consciousness. Goethe time and again stresses how nature by being separated from man is made into dead, depersonalized matter." [54]

Goethe, like Hegel, is very conscious of standing at the turning point of an old, classical world, and a new era of division and distortion of the clasical ideal. As a literary figure, he is the last to see Western man in his tragic and heroic greatness, at the end of his life witnessing the first phase of the historical process of dehumanization, which marks

---

[51]   J. Boehme, *De Signatura rerum*, I, 15.
[52]   Ernst Bloch, "Das Faustmotiv in der Phänomenologie des Geistes", *Hegel-Studien*, 159.
[53]   "Maximen und Reflectionen", *Werke* (Leipzig, n.d.), XX, no. 1062.
[54]   R. Huch, *op. cit.*, 129.

post-classical literature. As a man of science he fights vehemently (though in vain) for the understanding of nature as a cosmic unity in which man is physically and metaphysically integrated. "We are living at a time in which we are daily more and more urged to consider the two worlds to which we belong, the upper and the lower world, as united, in order to recognize the Idea in the real, and to silence our occasional displeasure with the finite by raising it to the infinite." [55]

Needless to say that in our technological society notions such as Idea and distinctions such as those between the lower and the upper world, the finite and the infinite, have lost all practical value. It will of course not do to put Goethe's metaphysics before us as a practical guide for overcoming the spirit of our 'two cultures'. Rather we must see in his efforts (and those of Schiller and Hegel) the impossibility of overcoming cultural estrangement other than in an abstract Idea.

That Richard Wagner should be included in this section in the company of Hegel may raise questions with those who automatically team him with Schopenhauer. The argument then is: Since Schopenhauer is Hegel's fiercest opponent, there can be no mental kinship between Hegel and Wagner. Wagner, no doubt, is fascinated with pessimistic world-views and moreover credits Schopenhauer with having inspired the libretto of Tristan. In a letter to Mathilde Wesendonk he speaks of Schopenhauer as of a friend whose thoughts transform his feelings and sorrows into a clear understanding: "clear perception cools our suffering".[56] The link between Wagner and Schopenhauer is obvious. In history, however, the obvious not infrequently is the least useful. For interesting though it may be to notice the prevalence of Will and the vague idea of cultural pessimism which links Wagner to Schopenhauer, Wagner's historical position in the nineteenth century is far more like that of Hegel. He shares with Hegel as well as Goethe the unique situation of standing at the close of the classical world, while at the same time preparing the post-classical developments. Wagner's music, with its manoeuvering of tonal variations and shifts, climaxes the process of the characteristic tonality of the classical era, yet prepares the way for the gradual emergence of a-tonal and serial music.

Strictly musically speaking, it may be argued that Beethoven is a more obvious representative to be put next to Hegel and Goethe. Wagner, however, owing to his poetic and essayistic writings, is not only historically a more rewarding source, he is also for the purpose of

[55]   Goethe, Maxim no. 1103.
[56]   Wagner to Mathilde Wesendonk, July 22, 1860, *Briefe*, V, 240.

this enquiry an unavoidable phenomenon. The search for totality, so fundamental for Hegel and Goethe is a no less important aspect of Wagner's work. Although no less critical of his age than they, Wagner's methods of curing the ills are entirely different. He by no means shies away from revolutions. On the contrary, he takes an active part in them, and when for this reason exiled from Germany, directs his revolutionary temper to a cultural restoration.

One of the first results is his essay on art and revolution, written in 1849 as a defiant manifesto and program for the future. Wagner, taking a dark view of contemporary dramatic art, which is entirely commercialized, focuses his attention on the theatre. It is managed by men trained in financial speculation, capitalists who see in their productions merely the means of accumulating capital. His revolution is the liberation of drama from industrial speculations; his program almost coincides with the Communist Manifesto. The tone is similar. The revolt against the capitalist system with Wagner, however, is not projected for the idea of the Proletariat, but for the idea of *Kunst*.[57]

Nietzsche has pointed out how Hegelian Wagner's life struggle is. Allowing for the pathological distortions in Nietzsche's judgments on Wagner, whether they be favorable or unfavorable, it is basically correct to say that Wagner meets Hegel on his own ground and tries to 'eternalize' the essence of Hegel's philosophy. Wagner is clearly unconscious of this. Nevertheless he is in a sense the heir of Hegel and his music the actualization of an Idea.[58] By the same token, however, it operates on similar premises as Goethe's writing which Nietzsche's irrational bias excludes from the evil of 'decadence'. The decadent to Nietzsche means an end-phase, and its representatives such as Plato, Hegel, or Wagner, are the great historical evildoers. Why Goethe in this conception should not be included, but rather be viewed as the epitome of 'health', is historically nonsensical, for Goethe, equally with Wagner, struggles for the total *Lebendige* the vitally organic whole. In *Das Kunstwerk der Zukunft* we hear a strong plea for vitality as the major condition for the restoration of art, inasmuch as the esthetic consolation lies in the fact that it can satisfy man's 'yearning for life'.[59] How badly Nietzsche could misread Wagner is also clear from a passage in another essay: "As the condition for the appearance of a work of art I

[57]   Wagner, "Die Kunst und die Revolution", *Gesammelte Schriften und Dichtungen* (Leipzig, 1872), III, 46.
[58]   Nietzsche, *op. cit.*, VIII, 33.
[59]   Wagner, *op. cit.*, III, 138.

set in the first place *Life*; not, however, the reflected life of philosophers and historians, but the most real, sensual life." [60] What could be more Goethean? What indeed could be more Nietzschean!

It is at this point that Wagner's importance as an analyst of cultural estrangement shows up. He sees that in his age the creeping threat of industrialization is reflected in the mechanization of society as a whole, and consequently will ultimately leave culture in a permanent state of ossification. Roughly eighty years before Ernst Jünger is to speak of the mobilization of the worker for the benefit of the technological age, Wagner senses that the machine is the dehumanizer of mankind. "The mechanical distinguishes itself from the artistic in that it goes from abstraction to abstraction, from means to means." [61] The artistic principle, on the contrary, deals with essentials, it disposes of means and of abstractions, in order to penetrate to the real source of all deductions, which is nature. The machine is the great benefactor of a luxury loving society, which has submitted human reasoning to technical refinement, and far from identifying itself with nature, has united itself with the mechanical process.

Man then, estranged from organically developed life, clings to the regutory principles of FASHION. "When we take the result for beginning, fulfilment for need, satisfaction for hunger, then movement and progress is only conceivable as an artificial need, when hunger is artificially stimulated. This indeed is the real stimulant of our present culture, and its form is – fashion." [62] By this of course is not meant the fashion which in every cultural development decides about social tastes or dress habits, but rather that social habit deprived of all personal and experienced preference, the pre-set taste, pre-fabricated for group use. This cultural fashion, the artificial stimulant is the 'most insane tyranny produced by human perversity'. Essentially it means absolute conformity, and its God is 'an egoistic, sexless impotent entity'. Its power lies in routine, namely routine as the indomitable despot of weak, cowardly and unreliable minds. Routine, in the sense of daily, pedestrian rut, according to Wagner, is the 'Communism of selfishness'.[63]

Wagner's arch-fiend is the *Philister*. This is the bourgeois merchant, the industrialist, the negation of all that art and culture stands for, the man who sells and buys art and culture, and exploits the artist. Wagner's

[60] "Eine Mittheilung an meine Freunde", *Ibid.*, IV, 297.
[61] "Das Kunstwerk der Zukunft", *Ibid.*, III, 71.
[62] *Ibid.*, 69.
[63] *Ibid.*, 70

revolution is fundamentally directed against the philistine, who is as
much the enemy of free culture as the absolute monarch is of democracy. He is 'the most ruthless and craven product of our civilization'.[64]
He is tolerant of everything, except that "which could remind him of
the fact that he ought to be human". The culture of the future has
nothing to expect from him. The real generator of art, indeed, the real
artist, will be the People. The people of course are not the mob. The
despised mob is not the normal product of true human nature, but
rather the artificial creation of the present unnatural civilization.[65] *Volk*
in Wagner's conception suggests the original, classless power of a nation,
which contains the seeds so to speak of cultural achievements and
historical greatness. The idea is clearly derived from Herder and the
notion of the *Volksgeist*. Insofar as it serves the cause of humanity it
has its *noblesse*, for humanity aims at cutting across class-lines and
natural borders. In this sense the concept of the people being the
generators of culture is impeccable.

It is easy to see, however, how such a program point can with the
minimum of change be manipulated into a most dangerous and vicious
political theory, one in flagrant contrast to the original ideal of cosmo-
politan humanity. The notion of the people then almost inconspicuously
changes into that of race with almost inevitable connotations of 'pure',
'healthy' and 'superior'. Eventually it may be implied that any minority
element is foreign and impure, and for that reason must be excluded
from the national benefits. How this policy can be pushed into the most
cruel and pernicious extremes we remember from the National Socialist
régime in Germany. Wagner himself in later utterances hints at this sort
of discrimination with his uncontrolled diatribes against the Jews. In
Das Kunstwerk der Zukunft his intentions are still purely cultural, with
side-swipes at the established reactionary governments of the time.
Indeed he uses the people of Israel as an example of a firmly integrated
power, creating its own historical destiny.

The notion of the *People* strongly indicates the pre-eminence of the
organic, that is the energy working from the inside towards manifestation. Just as the inner cohesion of a people alone can build a great
state, so the great work of art can be created only from an inner necessity. Meyerbeer's music is the epitome of the mechanical procedure
since it is put together by outer effects.[66] The real drama of the future

[64] *Ibid.*, IV, 281.
[65] *Ibid.*, III, 205.
[66] Wagner to Hanslick, Jan. 1, 1847, *Briefe*, XII, 80.

will not be influenced by outside forces; it is to be an organic being and becoming.[67] Like Hegel, Wagner aims at encompassing Western culture in all its expressions within an encyclopedic work. The *Gesamtkunstwerk* thus is a totality intended to overcome the disintegration of art and culture. There is always the element of the Savior in Wagner. He never tires of insisting on unity and cohesion as the factors which are to save the music drama. The esthetic attempt is, as with Schiller, a moral and social one as well. The purification of art is the redemption of society. For this reason his twin-guides are Apollo and Christ. Whereas the essays deal with the decline of opera and culture, in general, most of his libretti are concerned with the depravity of the world. The *Ring des Nibelungen* derives its dramatic intensity from the clash of the greed, lust and corruption of every one on the stage, excepting Brünhilde. Depravity has permeated all the regions of society: the religious order, that of the great capitalist, that of the proletariat from the depths. Wagner sees mankind "doomed in a world of racial and moral decay – a theme around which almost all of his later operas revolve".[68]

Wagner's solution for re-uniting the disintegrating world is the strange gift of his 'unending melody'. As 'metaphysical consolation', in Schopenhauer's words, it is naturally as useless in an increasingly mechanistic age as Hegel's absolute Idea, Faust's search for completeness, or Schiller's Esthetic State. Such metaphysical statements come at a time when the ACTUALITY of cultural integration has come to be recognized as a thing of the past.

3. EXPANSION: KIERKEGAARD, MARX, NIETZSCHE

Wagner, though not exactly fitting chronologically into the period of Hegel and Goethe, as we have noted belongs to them inasmuch as his encyclopedic view of the totality of culture and the search for a reconciling idea are in the foreground of his activities. The revolutionary quality of his work, however, makes him more akin to his own generation, which is that of Kierkegaard and Marx. We have already indicated how close Wagner is to Marx and Engels in his fulminations against commercial exploitation and in his promotion of the people against the tyranny of the bourgeois philistine. With Kierkegaard he

---

[67] Wagner, *op. cit.*, IV, 254.
[68] A. Dorpalen, in *Darwin, Marx and Wagner, a Symposium* (M. L. Plain, ed.) (Ohio State University, 1962), 7.

shares the conviction that the corruption of society is basically a religious one, and can only be redeemed by martyrdom and self-sacrifice, (symbolized in the figures of Senta, Elisabeth, Brünhilde, as well as Parsifal). While Wagner, however, rebels exclusively against specific institutions such as reactionary administrations, commercial opera theatres, and superficial styles of music, Kierkegaard and Marx both lay remarkable stress on the theoretical fight against a philosophical system, namely Hegel's metaphysics. While Wagner has little reason to oppose Hegel, as they both stand at the end of the classical era, Kierkegaard and Marx are the first events of the post-classical age.

Kierkegaard's importance for the history of cultural alienation lies, among other things, in the fact that he approaches the problem from the religious side. This of course is motivated not so much by a deliberate attempt on his part to be as efficient as possible, but by his natural disposition. As it is, however, his work seen as a whole is not only a revolt against Christianity, so that it may become religious again, but also, indirectly, an extremely intricate and subtle analysis of man's estrangement in the modern age. The most disparate critics of culture such as Eliot, Freud, or Toynbee, have considered religion as the nucleus of any culture. Indeed, however sceptically one may look at the position of established religions in history, it is undeniable that the unfolding of a civilization to its greatest heights of achievement is immediately connected with the vigor of its religion. It is for this obvious reason that Christianity constitutes the core of Hegel's work. Marx's attacks on Hegel's religious postulates demonstrate a deep-seated misunderstanding. If one regards Hegel's position, as Marx does, as the terminal of Western (Christian) civilization, from which vantage-point Hegel reviews its history, what else could Hegel possibly have done save to explain it as a Christian era and to evaluate it on its own terms, be it in a metaphysical translation?

Consequently, Kierkegaard's rebellion against Hegel is immediately relevant. Hegel's philosophical system, like the established Church, is a house of abstractions in which one cannot live. The philosophical Idea as the absolute reconciliation is the denial of man's inner reality: his authentic existence. But this existence, at least as Kierkegaard sees it, is a religious experience, intensified by an inherently human despair. Paradoxically it is this absolute despair which is to save him. Thus the fundamental savior-idea, that which for Hegel is the Idea for Goethe the organic *Ganze*, for Wagner artistic integration (*Gesamtkunstwerk*), for Marx the notion of Proletariat, is the Anxiety in Kierkegaard's work.

It is for this reason that in an age wherein man's estrangement from himself and his social context is emotionally expressed in terms of anxiety, Kierkegaard's appearance in history is uniquely significant. In the sense in which one has come to speak of the twentieth century as the 'age of anxiety', Kierkegaard is the prototype of modern man.

His modernity is exceedingly clear in *The Present Age* which, though written in 1846, is almost more applicable to the twentieth than to the nineteenth century. The age being without passion, it is, according to Kierkegaard, not stirred by an inner revolt. For a truly revolutionary temper moves to action. Ours is an age of advertisement and publicity.[69] At previous times men stood or fell by their actions; character was tested by what one did. Nowadays, Kierkegaard continues, "every one idles about and comes off brilliantly with the help of a little reflection, knowing perfectly well what ought to be done".[70] This passionless reflection results in the formalization of dialectic. "Dialectic leaves everything standing but cunningly empties it of significance." [71] Here Kierkegaard thinks of conceptional dialectic, especially that of Hegel; for the dialectic of the Either-Or is of a different order altogether. This is the dialectic of the entire existence, the real action, and indeed the real revolution. "If I am a genuine dialectician, if my very being is dialectic, then I should only find peace in the last Or." [72] The last Or to Kierkegaard is suffering.

Suffering understood in the creative sense, suffering caused by deep knowledge and deep experience, is no longer possible, for it requires a heroism which manifests itself only in positive ages. Our age, in Kierkegaard's thinking, kills both suffering and heroism by the process of levelling. This concept forms the core of *The Present Age*. It is one of the most characteristic trends of modern history, and Kierkegaard is one of the first to analyze it in full depth. Levelling is a silent and abstract way of avoiding upheavals. Indeed, its essence is abstract power, and its victory is one of abstraction over the individual. "The dialectic of the present age tends toward equality, and its most logical – though mistaken – fulfillment is levelling." [73] The work of levelling is thus related to the mechanization of society under the pressure of the growing power of the masses. This process cannot be arrested. The outlook for

---

[69]   Kierkegaard, *The Present Age*, 6.
[70]   *Ibid.*, 11.
[71]   *Ibid.*, 15.
[72]   *Journals*, 477.
[73]   *The Present Age*, 27, 28.

the future is dark. Individuals cannot halt this development because the age of heroism and chivalry is gone. Nor will society resist it, for it has put itself at the service of the power of abstraction. "The abstract levelling process, that self-combustion of the human race, . . . is bound to continue like a trade wind, and consume everything." [74]

Man's existence, that which makes him authentically man, is dehumanized into an abstract proposition. Values, instead of being relative ratios and representative tokens, have become the real thing. Hence our compulsive rush for money. What is sought after is the abstraction rather than what it represents. Abstraction thus sucks the life out of personal relationships. Consequently, "the springs of life, which are only what they are because of the qualitative differentiation of passion, lose their elasticity". [75]

In the course of his analysis Kierkegaard produces what I believe to be one of the most intricate and penetrating early descriptions of social estrangement. When the elasticity of the vital cohesion hardens, the social connections between 'opposites' grow abstract. Thus in the relationships between father and son, ruler and subject, teacher and pupil, the quality of respect and admiration may under the egalitarian principle vanish, leaving a situation in which two equals politely observe each other. The subject, for instance, no longer honors the ruler, or is angered by his ambitions. The relationship between the ruler and the citizen has lost its vitality, and the subject actually becomes a 'third party'. On this basis the institution of the committee becomes significant. "For a time committee after committee is formed, so long, that is to say, as there are still people who passionately want to be what they ought to be; but in the end the whole age becomes a committee." [76] The established order continues to exist, but more or less in abstractions. The relationship between father and son is levelled down, and though outwardly it may be irreproachable, it loses in strength of respect and devotion.

At the source of this discussion lies the difficult problem of authority. If one disposes of the autocratic authority of absolute monarchs, as Kierkegaard does, and enlightened monarchs become ineffectual, then the obvious alternative is the sovereignity of the people and popular consensus. But this to Kierkegaard leads to a new kind of despotism: the tyranny of the masses, the new Leviathan crushing the individual.

[74]   *Ibid.*, 32.
[75]   *Ibid.*, 16.
[76]   *Ibid.*, 17.

Although Kierkegaard is as vehement as Nietzsche in fighting the domination of the collective, he holds out no great hopes for the future. The battle against autocrats, against "princes and popes – and the nearer we come to our own times the truer this is – is easily compared with struggling against the masses, the tyranny of equality, against the grin of shallowness, nonsense, baseness, and bestiality".[77] Kierkegaard, rejecting both the conservative and liberal solutions, has no recourse save to declare all politics as harmful for the human character, and to respond to the actuality of the time by withdrawing into a self-imposed isolation.

The seclusion from reality, so typical for many of the great nineteenth-century figures, shows him basically a deficient disciple of his own doctrine. If the fundamental flaw of the age lies in reflective inaction, then Kierkegaard's own life is a vivid illustration of this inadequacy. To be sure, Kierkegaard's conception of action is the 'leap of enthusiasm' or the 'leap into the depth', which transcends actuality. But with this he steps into a metaphysical realm, and out of the very concrete situations of the age which he himself sets out to criticize. Essentially it seems that Kierkegaard's notion of the 'leap' is a replacement of Hegel's absolute Idea, only more mystically colored. It is once more an illustration of the remarkable tendency of the profoundest minds of the nineteenth century, while analyzing the very urgent and concrete troubles of the age, to resort for their solution to formulas in no way relevant to the scientific and technological setting to which man has to adjust himself.

Yet while this is a valid criticism of Kierkegaard's work; there is no denying that his exposure of a world of religious ossification, of social massification, and cultural mechanization, brilliantly reveals the situation of modern man. Kierkegaard's greatest fear for the future is of the individual bartering his freedom for the pseudo-security of conformity. "The individual no longer belongs to God, to himself, to his art or to his science, he is conscious of belonging in all things to an abstraction to which he is subjected by reflection, just as a serf belongs to an estate." [78] The new enslavement which Kierkegaard detects is an integral part of the alienation process. The separation from one self, or from one's original purpose and roots is caused by attachment to an extraneous world in a more or less permanent arrangement. The enslavement of modern man, according to Kierkegaard, occurs in his yielding

[77]   *Journals*, 502.
[78]   *The Present Age*, 29.

to uniformity, as he exchanges personal freedom for mass-opportunity, thus dissolving into the 'public'. The public, the 'monstrous abstraction', is nothing but a phantom, "developed with the help of the Press, which itself becomes an abstraction".[79] When the age grows analytic and reflective, that is when without enthusiasm or passion it destroys everything concrete, public opinion emerges as the ruling power.[80] It is remarkable to note how the meditative Kierkegaard who never resorts to invectives where persons are concerned, directs his most violent attacks against this abstract notion of the public. "The public is power in the basest possible way, power like bugs, or a stink ... A loathsome form of bloodlust, of thirsting for man's blood, not like a lion or a tiger – No, like a louse, like a legion of lice! The most disgusting of all tyrannies, the tyranny of the louse." [81]

The vehemence can only be explained by Kierkegaard's intense concern about the individual, who as the carrier of the consciousness of mankind, is being reduced to a part of a mechanism. Whether or not Kierkegaard is right, or perhaps is exaggerating his point, will be differently judged by different people. In the development of the nineteenth-century awareness of estrangement, however, he is undoubtedly one of the richest sources. A treatment like this must inevitably do injustice to the complexity of Kierkegaard's mind. By singling out one particular theme and tracing its historical development one risks the danger of schematizing cognate motifs into the background. Kierkegaard's analysis of human alienation is part of a far more widely ranging philosophy of existence in which man's historical destiny is at stake. Most of the nineteenth-century figures who have occupied themselves with the problem of alienation are complex, or controversial, or both. Some, like Wagner and Marx, have suffered from both unwarranted adulation and vilification, caused by their two-sided nature.

In spite of their complexities, Kierkegaard and Marx, however, are fairly single-minded in their reaction against Hegel. Karl Löwith in this respect has made it abundantly clear what Kierkegaard's and Marx's historical position is. Both invert Hegel's reconciliation of reason with reality. "Marx makes the political philosophy his aim, while Kierkegaard's attack is directed against philosophical Christendom." By doing so they not only dissolve Hegel's system, but at the same time the whole system of the bourgeois-Christian world. The philosophical foun-

---

[79]   Ibid., 37.
[80]   Ibid., 39.
[81]   Journals, 530.

dation of this radical critique of the actual world is the analysis of Hegel's idea of Reality as the 'unity of essence and existence'.[82] Whereas Kierkegaard isolates the ethical-religious theme, Marx concentrates on the economic-political questions. For Hegel, however, religion and nation are intimately related. The conception of God, according to him, constitutes the foundation of a people. Freedom within the constitutional arrangement "can only exist if the individuality is positively recognized in the divine ... It is for this reason that the nation is based on religion." [83] To Kierkegaard and Marx this statement is utterly fallacious. While the former claims religion for the individual only, the latter believes practical politics alone can serve the liberation of the collective The separation is significant. It indicates more than the future course of Existentialism and Dialectic Materialism. It tears the fabric of the historical bourgeois society.

Marx's theory of estranged labor, discussed in a previous chapter, seems to exhaust the topic of social alienation in his work. This is only formally so, however. For his writings as an entirety, including the extensive economic analysis of the *Capital*, aim at exposing the worker as isolated from the natural benefits of society. In the section on commodities in the *Capital* Marx discusses a form of alienation which he calls *Fetishism*, which points to the mysticism surrounding a commodity "because in it the social character of men's labor appears to them as an objective character stamped upon the product of that labor".[84] While there is a physical relationship between physical objects, this appears to be different with commodities. The existence of the commodity object and the value relation which stamps it as a commodity have no connection with its physical property. Fetishism is a magic, unreal quality which attaches itself to the products of labor as soon as they are produced as commodities. Since it has its origin in the 'peculiar social character of the labor' that produces commodities, fetishism actually is an extension of alienation of labor. The exchange value of commodities is in no way related to the aggregate of labor that goes into their production. Labor to the worker is something 'outside', it does not satisfy his own human need, but foremost a need lying outside the realm of his labor. The commodity, the product of his labor, is the 'objectified alienation' and production in the capitalist system is the alienation of the workers' activity.[85]

82   K. Löwith, *op. cit.*, 185.
83   Hegel, *Phil. der Geschichte, Einl.*, II, c.
84   Marx, *Capital*, I, i, 4.
85   H. Popitz, *op. cit.*, 170.

Since Marx's theory of social estrangement is identical with that of Hegel, there is no need here for further elaboration. It is only in the practical application that the difference between the two becomes evident. For Hegel the estrangement of the product of labor from the human existence producing the energy for that labor, can only be suspended in the realization of the Idea, that is, if one accepts realization as the essence of the absolute spirit which reveals itself in the phenomenal world. To Marx this is a topsy-turvy world-view which he dogmatically inverts. Real is only the physical, material, objective world. from which empirically ideas may be inferred. Since the alienation of need, product and labor is the specific result of the bourgeois way of running the social system, the cure simply lies in giving the apparatus into the hands of the working-class.

Within the framework of this enquiry we need not enter into the debate on the validity of Marx's economic and political conclusions in general. From the point of view of alienation, however, it is clear that it apparently does not make any difference whatever whether the bourgeois producer or the proletariat runs the social machine. In either case the estrangement as dehumanization remains. Why is this? The answer is as simple as obvious. Marx, like Kierkegaard, demonstrates cogently and masterfully how man in the bourgeois structure is mechanized into an abstraction. We are thus entitled to expect some sort of social remedy which is to restore that organic human quality which Goethe derives from physics, the human totality. But how, one may ask, is this restoration, the *Aneignung*, as Marx calls it, to work for the liberation of the laborer if the machine far from being dismantled, is going to be adjusted (streamlined) to a new ownership, the bureaucratic committee?

Having followed Hegel most of the way, and rightly and correctly ascribed the enslavement of the working class to the system of private property, he then advocates an emancipation under the aegis of the state-system. The private producer is replaced by the *particrat*, Hegel's ideology of the Spirit by the Proletariat. Marx, like Kierkegaard, all his life combats the danger of abstraction for the survival of man's humanity. Yet few of the nineteenth-century writers are as theoretically analytic as is Marx, and few indulge so persistently in abstractions. For what else is the proletariat but an abstraction in Marx's mind? How does the proletariat operate? How does it make revolution? How does it run a socialist state? We know the historical answers. The proletariat indeed does not do any of these things. The party bosses operate it. The intellectuals make revolution. The dictator runs the proletarian state.

Writing about Proudhon, Marx indirectly makes his own intended position clear. "Instead of the practical and violent actions of the masses, which alone can bring the solution to these conflicts: instead of this comprehensive, continual and complicated movement, Mr. Proudhon puts the movement of emptying his head (*le mouvement cacadauphin*) . . . Now you see why Mr. Proudhon is the declared enemy of all revolutionary movement. The solution of the present problems to him does not lie in public action, but in the dialectic circulation within his brains." [86] To Marx only violence and revolution is practical political action for the sake of the working class. Not the social experiments of Fourier and Owen, not the specific program points of the various socialist parties in nineteenth-century Europe. Only revolution. It is this dogmatism which points to the abstract nature of Marx's message. Now it is not the absolute Spirit which appears as the dialectic synthesis, nor Lessing's religious revelation, Schiller's esthetic revelation, or Fichte's revelation of the world-spirit, but the revelation of the proletarian revolt.[87]

How absolutely authoritarian this ideology is becomes evident from Marx's violent attitude toward anything that theoretically may be in the way of the fulfilment of the socialist state. One of these barriers he believes is formed by the Jews. In his essays on the upheavals in France, the articles on 'the Jewish question', and in his letters to Engels the Jews are invariably indentified with usury, greed and exploitation of the poor. In the *Deutsche Ideologie* he tells us that it is the circumvention of law which makes "the religious Jew a religious Jew".[88] In the *Deutsch-Französische Jahrbücher* of 1843 the principle of Judaism is presented as egoism.[89] "The chimerical nationality of the Jew is the nationality of the merchant, the money-maker." If society could succeed in doing away with the usurer and his premises, the Jew would be made impossible. Hence "the social emancipation of the Jews is the liberation of society from the Jews".[90]

To what extent these and other anti-semitic utterances are merely personal or express something inherent in Dialectic-Materialism must be left undiscussed here. It is not difficult to see, however, how in this radical creed lies the doctrinal justification for purge terrors such as Stalin found it necessary to organize. It would be an error, however, to

---

86   Marx to P. W. Annenkow, Dec. 28, 1846, *Werke* (Berlin, 1963), XXVII, 460.
87   H. Popitz, *op. cit.*, 170.
88   *MEGA*, V, 162.
89   *Ibid.*, I, 1, 603.
90   *Ibid.*, 604, 606.

conclude, as has frequently been done, that Marx is a soulless fanatic without fundamental human considerations. He is not. His character and his work are complex and cannot be judged on the strength of partial manifestations. As far as the theme of estrangement is concerned, the restoration of the humanity of man through a proletarian revolution is proved to be a failure within the communist confines themselves. Reports from East European countries indicate that nothing could be more estranged from 'reality' than life under the Communist dispensation, and that this fact is felt more and more painfully by the post-war generation. According to an account of the *New York Times* of January 20, 1965, the efforts of government officials to suppress public expression of this feeling of unrest have been given up. The new intellectual Communist declares openly that the alienation suffered in a worker's republic is caused by the bureaucratic régime which has replaced the private exploiter. Mihajlo Markovic, a university professor in Belgrade, thinks that Communism "has created a professional bureaucracy that treats people as things". Consequently various proposals are being suggested to 'humanize' Communism. The recognition of this need comes a little late it seems. It is also futile. The organization of the proletariat in Marx's terms already implies dehumanization inasmuch as all massification turns the human being into an abstraction. Marx's formula for overcoming alienation indeed, is itself a textbook example of the workings of the alienated mind.

Whereas Marx approaches the problem of estrangement as a real Hegelian, and Kierkegaard treats it at least with an Hegelian consciousness of dialectics, with Nietzsche (that is after *The Birth of Tragedy*) we have to do with an entirely new brand of philosophy: reasoning 'with the hammer'. In *Ecce homo* we are told "I am the most terrible man who has existed so far . . . My desire to destroy equals my power to destroy . . . I am the first Immoralist: in this I am the Destroyer *par excellence*." [91] Philosophizing, heretofore handled with deft instruments now, with Nietzsche, becomes a matter of unrestricted subjectivity, indeed, a source of intellectual violence. As a result, not only thinking with sledgehammers has become fashionable, but also ideological dynamiting is a successful approach, which on Nietzsche's principle has "blown the world apart".[92] Thinking with fury and outrage is a timely

---

[91]   Nietzsche, *Werke* (Kröner, ed.), XV, 118.
[92]   K. Löwith, "Friedrich Nietzsche nach sechzig Jahren", *Gesammelte Abhandlungen* (Stuttgart, 1960), 132.

activity. Not only does it fit in well with the new political violence as suggested by Sorel's *Reflections on Violence*, it is soon to be revealed in Expressionist drama and painting, in the primitivism of sculpture, in the pluri-tonal stridencies of modern music. The cult of the ignoble savage has come to be a part of twentieth-century culture. It is not so much that there is more terror in the streets or in the intellectual's way of handling contemporary issues, as that the concept of the violence itself is accepted as a legitimate tool for artistic, political and social success.

Both Syndicalism and Fascism have learned from Nietzsche. National Socialism expresses itself in a Super-terror by which it practices the new re-evaluation of moral values. Yet, in spite of this, it would be misleading to present Nietzsche as a proto-Fascist. His disgust at German chauvinism and Teutonic power stupidity alone makes him an enemy of all that the Hitler régime stands for. He would have been as appalled by Nazi politics as he was by those of the Socialists. Like Kierkegaard he is neither a liberal nor a conservative. Nietzsche's thinking goes beyond the range of political theories, and it is absolutely untenable to evaluate his writing in terms of partisan politics as American critics tend to do. The scope of his philosophical nihilism is so radical that in its sweep all political platforms and indeed all political actions vanish. Practical politics, like practical Christianity, involve at least the illusion of moral standards. Morality, however, is the arch-foe of the new nihilism. Inasmuch as we believe in morality we condemn life.[93]

Nietzsche's nihilism is absolute, and he believes it is going to be the history of the next few centuries. But it should be understood as a 'pathological intermezzo', the premise of the idea of the 'eternal recurrence'. This nihilism is an inverted yearning for eternity, the undertow as strong in Nietzsche's writings as in Wagner's 'eternal melody'. The re-evaluation of Nietzsche's thought, which starts around 1935 with studies by Jung, Löwith, Jaspers and Heidegger, helps us to understand Niezsche as the spokesman of the modernity of our age, which gradually comes to think in terms of a total destruction of the centuries old Christian and moral code, regardless of what may come of it. Nietzsche rejects historical Christianity and Western morals because they deny the essence of life. As a disciple of Goethe he draws the desparate conclusion that the fulness and health of human existence can be retained only by totalitarian destruction of the weak and humble (conclusions which, needless to say, would have terrified Goethe).

[93] *Wille zur Macht*, Aph. 4, 6.

The similarity between Nietzsche's and Kierkegaard's nihilist concepts are too obvious to go by unnoticed. Kierkegaard's nihilism is a conscious leap into Nothingness, and the transcending liberation, expressed categorically in the idea of Repetition, is illustrated in Job's experience with the Voice in the whirlwind. Repetition is related to Nietzsche's Eternal Recurrent, in which the total annihilation overcomes itself. Whereas Kierkegaard, however, presents Repetition as a personal experience, Nietzsche prophesies a cultural event from which the Superman will arise. Whereas Kierkegaard criticises his age because he believes that its trends conspire against the individual, (the religiously elect), Nietzsche's *Zeitkritik* is itself part of the destructive process needed in the cycle of recurrent life.

The forms of progress on which the eighteenth and nineteenth centuries pride themselves are merely manifestations of decadence to Nietzsche. Modern humanity is a thickly quilted coat, and our modern 'virtues' represent nothing but a decline of vitality.[94] His attacks against the modernity of liberalism are no less devastating than those against conservative religion. Liberalism is a degeneration process, turning men into herd-animals. The whole Western world (except Russia) has lost those instincts from which Future can grow. "One lives for the present, one lives very fast, – one lives very irresponsibly, precisely this one calls Freedom." [95] People think they risk slavery if they mention the word authority. Goethe's championing of the strong and complete appears to be useless since the modern age (referring back to the eighteenth century with its hyper-sentimentality, its effeminate taste, and socialist politics) is an age of sickness and decline.[96] Here Nietzsche takes up a theme on which Schiller before him had touched. But for Nietzsche there is no esthetic or educational scheme for overcoming the decadence. There is no remedy save the beneficial destruction of Christian morality.

Nietzsche and Kierkegaard belong to the twentieth rather than the previous century, and both are defiantly conscious of their superior insight into the nature of the age, as a terminal of a thousand years' development.[97] Inevitably they are lone prophets and little understood in their own time. Their decisive significance can be fully assessed only in a century when man through cruel experiences has learned to face inevitable facts. Others, as noted, are able to see the deep historical

---

[94] "Götzendämmerung", *Werke*, VIII, 146-147.
[95] *Ibid.*, 151.
[96] *Ibid.*, 164.
[97] K. Jaspers, *Vernunft und Existenz* (München, 1960), 30.

meaning of the nineteenth century before it is over, but none except Kierkegaard and Nietzsche LIVE their own writings. Kierkegaard and Nietzsche suffer intellectual martyrdom by existentially going through the estrangement which they analyze. As a 'lived' philosophy their thought upsets the basic premises of historical philosophy of the Western world, and both find their great example in that other 'decadent', Socrates. It is precisely as 'decadent' thinkers that Kierkegaard and Nietzsche are able to expose the process of disintegration which they see growing in their age. They also are remarkable for the fact that they do not offer esthetic, philosophical or political remedies for the disturbing fact of alienation. If man is becoming separated from himself, no amount of outside help will arrest the process. On the contrary, in order to return to himself, man must experience his destiny to the full until the Zero-point where Despair and Repetition, Destruction and Eternal Recurrence become identical.

It is self-evident that such a message is not meant to cater to the popular market, as do such successful world movements as ecumenical Christianity, Dialectic Materialism, the organization of the United Nations, or the international brotherhood of Moslems. Kierkegaard and Nietzsche far from offering a creed, set out to destroy all premises of a creed. Their message is simply a historical statement on the 'situation Man' in the modern age.

4. UNITED STATES: EMERSON, THOREAU, MELVILLE

The study of the emergence and development of alienation has chiefly been a European concern, which is not surprising in view of the fact that its sources lie in the outstanding nineteenth-century writers of the Continent. Important social and cultural changes, however, rarely occur other than universally. Although their appearance may not be recognized everywhere at the same time, be met with the same emotional response, and consequently not be discussed in the same expressive terms, culture as an epochal configuration can hardly be divided by national boundaries. Human estrangement, as we think of it today, is a general concern of the Western world. Local or national situations may accentuate some of its aspects more than others, but the discussion, especially after the second World War, is clearly international.

In the United States this concern has been stimulated by various outside forces such as Existentialism and Marxism, but it would be shortsighted to overlook the possible native traditions. Since cultural alienation is rooted in the problems of industrialization, mechanization, massification, conformism, and similar social trends, the United States seems a most rewarding terrain for this enquiry. It follows that the American Transcendentalist writings, which coincide with the growing recognition of man's estrangement on the Continent of Europe, will be the most likely place to look for concurrent thoughts. And this the more so inasmuch as Transcendentalism draws considerably on European contemporaries.

In France the intellectual climate of the time never seems to favor a real encounter with the problems of alienation. To be sure, there is a considerable amount of social critique expounded in the works of Saint-Simon, Fourier, or Proudhon, to name a few of the early representatives of Socialism. There is a probing of the spirit of the age by Chateaubriand, Bonal, and Joseph de Maistre. But their basically reactionary efforts to reconstruct the past glories of the Middle Ages disregard the entirely new social and industrial structure in which man must find his place. One can also point to the growing trend of pessimism, which from the Romantics through Baudelaire to Flaubert's *Correspondance* indeed relates to a criticism of the age. But it is by its very nature too onesidedly negative to recognize the realities of alienation, which, as we have noted, has a dialectic structure.

Why the intelligence of the French mind can overlook for so long the phenomena of estrangement is difficult to explain. The political and revolutionary events in France show more or less the same pattern as elsewhere on the Continent, and the growing consciousness of the collective over against individuality here follows the common trend. The only suggestion one might make is that the absence of the natural dialectic disposition prevents the French mind from seeing the dialectic tendencies of the nineteenth century. There is of course a fairly important group of thinkers in France who adopt Idealist and dialectic methods. But these are imported straight from Germany, and in spite of their relative success, they seem to be grafted onto the traditional stem without ever becoming an integral part of the native growth. The psychological theories of Maine de Biran, with the stress on volition take their lead from Kant, and the famous slogan "I will, therefore I am", makes him a fitting contemporary of Schopenhauer. The most important figure in this connection, however, is Victor Cousin, who is influenced by Fichte's I-Non-I formula, and in general promotes German Idealism in France. He is also one of the important links with

American Transcendentialism. George Ripley includes him in the *Specimens of Foreign Standard Literature* (1838) and writes about Cousin's work: "We need a philosophy like this to purify and enlighten our politics, to consecrate our industry, to cheer and elevate society." [98]

The second link between Continental thinking and the men of Concord has long been recognized in the English Romanticists. Coleridge especially tries to make German speculative thought popular in Britain, and in New England he is immediately accepted as a congenial mind. With Wordsworth he visits Germany, meets some of the Romantic writers and returns with a few of Schelling's works which are to have a profound influence on him. By intuition he is able to see the essential problems of the time, but his mind often rambles off into a confusion of inconsequential details. More than any of his countrymen he is aware of the growing cracks in the contemporary civilization which "is a corrupting influence".[99] He distinguishes varnished from polished people, civilization from culture, the latter being "the harmonious development of those qualities and faculties that characterize our humanity". Thus a nation can never be too cultivated, but may easily become an over-civilized race.[100] The contrast culture versus civilization is only one of many with which he likes to play. They are part of the Romanticist's nature, but are definitely stimulated by the polarities of German Idealist thought. So is for instance the Kantian distinction between Reason and Understanding which occurs in Coleridge's *Aids to Reflection*, and which Emerson borrows in his essay on Nature. So is his differentiation between person and citizen which suggests a rift between man as a living organism in the natural cohesion of his community and man as a political constituent of the collective power. Whatever we can do for the future society or the future state, can only originate in the consciousness of the self: "We must be men in order to be citizens." [101]

Coleridge's concern with man's organic place in culture, stripped of its encumbering religious speculations, vaguely recognizes the split which at the time is widening between culture as an enlightening educational, and perfecting process, and one merely luxurious and outwardly glittering. In this he goes further than Wordsworth, who himself is certainly not without critical insights into the weakening structure of his

---

[98] Quoted in O. B. Frothingham, *Transcendentalism in New England* (New York, 1876), 74.
[99] Coleridge, "On the Constitution of the Church and State", *Complete Works* (New York, 1853), VI, 51.
[100] *Ibid.*, 55.
[101] *Ibid.*, 51.

age. In his sonnets Wordsworth can speak of England as a 'fen of stagnant waters', full of selfish men who need the majesty of Milton's view, and, unmoved by the beauty of nature, give their hearts away as 'a sordid boon', he can realize the problem of the individualistic poet and his duties towards the community,[102] or announce with pride his re-conversion to the world, accepting society as 'his glittering bride'.[103] But his confident optimism never allows him to coexist for long with an unresolved conflict between society and solitude, as is Emerson's lot. Shelley and Byron are stirred by a strong social revolt, and following William Godwin's *Enquiry concerning Political Injustice* fight the good, but rather ineffectual, fight against the corruption of their society. Their rebellion is directed against incidental, if crass, injustices, at best against a system that must be replaced. They are not aware of deeper causes behind the exploitation of the lower and the corruption of the upper classes. Coleridge alone during the early decades of the century has an insight, if only a nebulous one, into the historical estrangement of man from his culture.

Besides the German and English influences which work on the Transcendentalist mind there are a number of other tributaries, from Platonic idealism and Oriental thought, to puritan moral integrity which supply and feed the American Renaissance. It is above all the robust originality of most of the Transcendentalists which gives them their unique place in American history, and elevates American literature to the classical level. The decades of Transcendentalist prevalence, the 'Golden Age' of American culture, are also unique in another respect. Most periods of great bloom show their artistic and literary achievements to be an indirect confirmation of the particular style and character of an age. It is not difficult to see that Pindar's odes and Sophocles' tragedies confirm the splendor of Athens at its height. The geometrical clarity of Descartes, Racine or Molière belongs inseparably to the administrations of Richelieu and Louis XIV. The spirit of Rembrandt, Hals, Grotius and Huyghens is allied with the free Dutch Republic, and the works of Goethe, Schiller and Herder reflect the Humanist climate of Karl August's court at Weimar. In contrast, the work of Emerson Melville, Thoreau, Whitman and Hawthorne, though thoroughly American in nature, is for a considerable part a reaction, if not a revolt against an age which is marked by the unmistakable uniqueness of American enterprise.

[102] Wordsworth, *Resolution and Independence*.
[103] Wordsworth, *The Excursion*, III.

What actually the Transcendentalist era confirms most of all is the opposition of two strong native forces: the self-reliance of the individual against the conformity of a modern industrial order. It is the fundamental problem to which most of the troubles which disturb the historical society of the United States, can be traced. To say that the Transcendentalist mind is against materialism, against society, or against politics is an erroneous over-simplification. Its exclusive enemy is simply the attitude which does injustice to the freedom of human dignity and integrity. Such a detrimental attitude may stem from dogmatic formalism, ritualism, political machinery, – anything which takes man away from his natural roots, and instead of cultivating the free expansion of his individual self, makes him a part of a mechanized whole, be it religious, social, or political.

Emerson's lectures come as a voice in the wilderness. In the bustling excitement of the industrializing cities and frontier towns he appears as "a flute-player, one who plucks his reeds in the Concord river".[104] His misty Platonism is far over the heads of his audiences, and the pundits and intellectuals of Boston dismiss him as a pantheist and his message as 'conceited, laborious nonsense'.[105] He goes his way as a solitary prophet, with his public listening though not understanding. And when after his long life all is said and done, the wrongs which he means to set right have increased and spread with the social expansion. In his lecture *On the Times* of 1841, he diagnoses the disease of the age as the 'Uncertainty as to what we ought to do'.[106] There is a deep distrust of our activity, "a great perplexity hangs like a cloud on the brow of all cultivated persons, a certain imbecility in the best spirits, which distinguishes the period". Whereas our forefathers did not see beyond the need of the present, we are self-conscious. "They planted their foot strong and doubted nothing. We mistrust every step we take. We find it the worst thing about time that we know not what to do with it." [107]

This criticism seems on the surface rather unjustified in view of the outward appearance of American life at that time, filled as it is with energy and enterprize to conquer the seemingly infinite space of the West. But this according to Emerson's Idealism represents only a material fulfilment and will never satisfy man's spiritual aspirations. While he becomes the victor of space, he goes astray in time. He is a

104 Van Wyck Brooks, *The Flowering of New England* (New York, 1955), 204.
105 Everett, quoted in Van Wyck Brooks, *Ibid.*, 203.
106 Emerson, *Complete Works* (Boston, 1895), I, 268.
107 *Ibid.*

stranger in time, and time is a 'masquerade of Eternities'.[108] It has its roots in an invisible, spiritual reality. Emerson's message has an unreal ring in the pragmatic reality of the expansionist world. Being estranged in time to him means having lost a purpose, a direction towards goals which fulfill the entire human being. But how is this state of mind going to be remedied, when the exclusive direction of modern man is towards the fulfilment of greed?

Instead of the old "Repent ye!" his gospel is one of Reform! "What is a man born for but to be a Reformer, a Re-maker of what man has made; renouncer of lies; a restorer of truth and good, imitating that great Nature which embosoms us all?" [109] Man must renounce all that is not true to him. He must refind himself in solitude. Why must he be rich? Why must he be under the continuous pressure of having to spend incomes? It is for cake that we run into debt. It is not our mind, our vision, our friendship, our love that cost so much. "Our expense is almost all for conformity." [110] Why is modern man in a perpetual rush for possessions? The answer is: only for want of thought. "We dare not trust our wit for making our house pleasant to our friend, and so we buy ice-creams." [111]

Emerson never tires of pointing to solitude as the purifier of the soul; solitude where man must retire (temporarily?) from society to restore his dignity. His essay on *Self-reliance* is the classical document on the intensifying awareness of the threat of dehumanization in conformity. To him it seems that the new society is conspiring against each of its members. It is a "stock-company, in which the members agree, for the better security of his bread to each shareholder, to surrender the liberty and culture of the eater. The virtue in most request is conformity. Self-reliance is its aversion. It loves not realities and creators, but names and customs." [112] The essay as a whole is a Romantic paean to the Great Man, who is misunderstood, defies conformity, and "in the midst of the crowd keeps with perfect sweetness the independence of solitude".[113] It is also with its majestic but sweeping rhetorics a rather misleading guide to Emerson's thought in general. For the bitter attack on the leveling effects of society is by no means his last word on the problem. He is no anarchist. He will fervently defend the authenticity

[108]   *Ibid.*, I, 247.
[109]   *Ibid.*, I, 236.
[110]   *Ibid.*, I, 232.
[111]   *Ibid.*, I, 233.
[112]   *Ibid.*, II, 51.
[113]   *Ibid.*, II, 55.

of the individual inasmuch as he equates it with the dignity of humanity. But he is not prepared to abandon society's structure, or to undermine it with wild revolutionary schemes. He finds safety in 'the diagonal line'. In *Society and Solitude* he declares that all the conditions will be met if we can only keep our independence, yet not lose our sympathy. "Society and solitude are deceptive terms. It is not the circumstance of seeing more or fewer people, but the readiness of sympathy, that imports." [114] The Self-reliance of the individual will serve society by deriving basic principles from its own insights, and accepting society as the natural element where they are to be applied.

Emerson's chief objectives remind one of his contemporary Kierkegaard. Without the Dane's nervous energy, intricate subtleties, and thorough education, Emerson yet resembles Kierkegaard in the deep analysis of the age, and the conviction that society can only be saved from the onslaught of materialistic industrialization by the strength of the unrestricted individual. Cultivation of the individual is the real culture to Emerson. Culture means the sum of influences that go to "refine and redeem the raw egoism of the natural man".[115] The true test of a great civilization lies not in military power, or economic statistics, it is "not the consensus, nor the size of cities, nor the crops – no, but the kind of man the country turns out".[116] In this trust in the educational power of culture for the restoration of humanity, Emerson appears in an eighteenth-century light, and is quite unlike Kierkegaard for whom the individual can only maintain himself in a radical conversion through Dread. Is it perhaps in this difference that we must look for the reason why, while Kierkegaard's work starts a trend of expanding thought which, in revised versions, is to continue to question man's alienation in later times, Emerson's message (along with all the other Transcendental efforts) stirs no further repercussions? His seems to be a rather amiable reaching which analyzes the nature of the age acutely, but somehow does not penetrate into the obscure vistas of the future.

Emerson can live quietly with the split between man and the collective. He endures the strain between the two and has no intention of giving up one for the other. Thoreau is different. Thoreau is unable to adopt a rather halfhearted citizenship. He enacts so to speak the separation of individual and community by LIVING the former com-

[114]   *Ibid.*, VII, 20.
[115]   S. E. Whicher, *Freedom and Fate: an Inner Life of Ralph Waldo Emerson* (Philadelphia, 1953), 84.
[116]   Emerson, *op. cit.*, VII, 34.

pletely and by cutting practically all ties with society. He chooses "not to live in this restless, nervous, bustling, trivial Nineteenth Century, but stand or sit thoughtfully while it goes by".[117] From the sidelines he watches the developing industrial order. Like Emerson he notices that man is no longer true to himself. He lives a pattern, an image of life rather than his own life. "Through an infirmity of our natures, we suppose a case, and put ourselves into it, and hence are in two cases at the same time, and it is doubly difficult to get out." [118] For the most part, accordingly, we "are not what we are". We have taken a false position. Probably without knowledge of Schiller, Hegel and Marx, he deplores the alienation of the laborer: "Actually, the laboring man has not leisure for a true integrity day by day; he cannot afford to sustain the manifest relations to men; his labor would be depreciated in the market. He has no time to be anything but a machine." [119]

The factory machine, however, is not the only enemy. Man is badly trapped in the mechanism of the whole society. The adjustment to this mechanism has brought him to a state of 'quiet desperation'. Unlike Kierkegaard for whom despair is existential and therefore inherent in the human situation, Thoreau believes that it is a product of social interdependence. "A stereotyped but unconscious despair is concealed even under what are called the games and amusements of mankind." [120] Relief from desperation can be obtained only by releasing oneself from the slavery of the social institutions. It is especially the wage system which makes man a slave of his community. The way one may get money leads without exception downward. If you want to be paid as a writer or lecturer, "you must be popular, which is to go down perpendiculary. Those services which the community will most readily pay for, it is most disagreeable to render. You are paid for being something less than a man." [121]

In the false coherence of society politics plays a major role. To the Transcendentalist the politician is one who barters his freedom for popularity. Instead of relying on the power of his own freely developed self, he manipulates outside forces. Emerson believes that the politician assumes more power than belongs to him; "more power than is the legitimate attraction of his faculty. He must pay for that excess and

---

[117] *Walden* (New York, 1946), 366.
[118] *Ibid.*, 365.
[119] *Ibid.*, 7.
[120] *Ibid.*, 9.
[121] "Life without Principle", *Ibid.*, IV, 458-459.

truckle for it." [122] Thoreau puts the problem more sharply by relating it to the national consciousness of freedom. The United States is said to be the nation of liberty. But what kind of liberty are we cultivating? Thoreau doubts that we can restrict ourselves to a political freedom. "Even if we grant that the American has freed himself from a political tyrant, he is still the slave of an economical and moral tyrant. We are born free, but we have not yet learned to live free. What is the value of any political freedom but as a means to moral freedom?" [123]

The sharp distinction between moral and political liberty is a modern tendency characteristic of the new consciousness, and one which, as we have noted, is especially pronounced in Schiller's work. Moral freedom to Thoreau is the highest guarantee for individuality. We have settled the *res-publica*, now the task for the Americans is to establish the *res-privata*. The historical process from monarchy to democracy is a process toward respect for the individual. "There will never be a free and enlightened State until the State comes to recognize the individual as a higher and independent power, from which all its own power and authority are derived, and treats him accordingly." [124] Time and again in his essay *Civil Disobedience* Thoreau uses the simile of the machine to indicate his disdain for the organized state. "If the injustice is part of the necessary friction of the machine of government, let it go, let it go: perchance it will wear smooth . . . but if it is such a nature that it requires you to be the agent of injustice to another, then, I say, break the law. Let your life be a counter-friction to stop the machine." [125] The masses serve the state not as men, but as machines,[126] and echoing Coleridge almost exactly, Thoreau believes that we "should be men first, and subjects afterwards".[127]

The first essential which Thoreau pursues is a full life, which is one in communion with nature. Saluting the flag and casting a vote are puny accidentals. Like the early Christians "he is far too religious a man to commit the idolatry of saluting a symbol of secular power . . . The things which his contemporaries take for the supreme realities of life, matter, money and political rights, have only an instrumental use for Thoreau." [128] First essentials certainly do not include rights. Voting is

[122]   Emerson, "Aristocracy", *op. cit.*, X, 50.
[123]   Thoreau, *op. cit.*, IV, 477.
[124]   "Civil Disobedience", *Ibid.*, IV, 387.
[125]   *Ibid.*, IV, 368.
[126]   *Ibid.*, 359.
[127]   *Ibid.*, 358.
[128]   Lewis Mumford, "The Golden Day", from *Thoreau: a Collection of Critical*

"a sort of gaming, with a slight moral tinge to it, a playing with right and wrong, with moral questions".[129] Precisely this toying with right and wrong is what distinguishes the political rights (of voting) from moral freedom, which is an absolute right. Voting to Thoreau's reasoning, especially in a majority-rule system, thrives on the leveling of individuals. The vote of a thoughtful and convinced man avails nothing against a majority of blind followers. "There is but little virtue in the action of masses of men. When the majority shall at length vote for the abolition of slavery, it will be because they are indifferent to slavery, or because there is but little slavery left to be abolished by their vote. *They* will then be the only slaves. Only *his* vote can hasten the abolition of slavery who asserts his own freedom by his vote." [130]

There is no need here to point to possible flaws in this theory, or to suggest that radical individualism, however well intended may easily lead to unbridled selfishness, and an a-moral social Darwinism.[131] The important point in our context is the concern for the fact that political liberty if exercized thougthlessly reverses itself and actually becomes moral slavery. To what extent this really happens in Thoreau's time, and is true in ours, is another matter. The Transcendentalist, just as clearly as Schiller, Marx and Kierkegaard, sees that the integrity of humanity is at stake, and that something must be done about safe-guarding its increasingly constricted freedom. How valid their disparate remedies are is a question which lies outside the confines of this study.

With *Moby Dick* American literature rises to its greatest maturity and profundity. The work is also the most moving and astonishing state-ment of human estrangement in the English language. The name of its narrator, Ishmael, already indicates the psychological climate of the outcast who "dwelt in the wilderness".[132] That Ishmael is as much a fugitive from society as is, for instance, Thoreau, with adventurous oceans replacing gentle Walden Pond, is immediately made clear on the first page. "Whenever I find myself growing grim about the mouth; whenever it is a damp, drizzly November in my soul; whenever I find

---

Essays, Sherman Paul, ed. (Englewood Cliffs, 1962), 16.
[129] Thoreau, *op. cit.*, IV, 363.
[130] *Ibid.*, 363-364.
[131] To suggest that Thoreau is in any way related to Social Darwinism as H. Eulau does in "Wayside Challenger", *Thoreau: a Collection of Critical Essays*, 127, seems absolutely unwarranted.
[132] *Genesis*, 21: 20.

myself involuntarily pausing before coffin warehouses, and bringing up
the rear of every funeral I meet; and especially whenever my hypos gets
such an upper hand of me, that it requires a strong moral principle to
prevent me from deliberately stepping into the street, and methodically
knocking people's hats off – then I account it high time to go to sea
as soon as I can." [133] And amiable as is his character, Ishmael has no
friends except Queequeg, a miserable 'isolato' from the South Sea.
Ishmael is the 'outsider' in the story, yet in a sense more involved than
any of the other characters. As such he represents the human consciousness, the only survivor of the ultimate catastrophe.

Moby Dick clearly has a multiple narrative, but it is above all a
story of the sea. Melville leaves no doubt about the centrality of its
function. Ishmael and the sea belong together as awareness and psyche.
The sea is the independence from the bonds of society which the main-
land represents to Ishmael. The separation from the home-land is
realized as "a mortally intolerable truth; that all deep earnest thinking
is but the intrepid effort of the soul to keep the open independence of
her sea; while the wildest winds of heaven and earth conspire to cast
her on the treacherous, slavish shore".[134] Nothing could put Melville's
thinking more firmly into the Transcendentalist orbit. Nothing could
better express the plight of the individual who, detached from his native
soil, witnesses the inexorable catastrophic end of his futile pursuit.

But Ishmael is no mere observer. For the very fact that he is this
deep consciousness makes him sheer reflection on the course of the
events. "The burden of his thought, the essential cause of his estrangement, is that he cannot come to any conclusion about anything." [135]
This represents Ishmael's pivotal function in the epic, and makes him,
and by implication the narrative, so pre-eminently modern. "For him
nothing is ever finally settled and decided; he is man, or as we like to
think, modern man, cut off from the certainty that was once his inner
world. Ishmael no longer has any sure formal belief. All is in doubt,
all is in eternal flux, like the sea. "And so condemned, like 'all his race
from Adam down', to wander the seas of thought, far from Paradise,
he now searches endlessly to put the whole broken story together, to
find a meaning." [136] Although the physical events obviously deal with
Ahab and his search for the whale, the metaphysical overtones are all

[133] Melville, "Moby Dick", *Works*, Standard Ed. (London, 1922), VII, 1.
[134] *Ibid.*, 133.
[135] Alfred Kazin, *Introduction to Moby Dick* (Boston, 1956), vii.
[136] *Ibid.*, viii.

provided by Ishmael's reflections. What Melville does through him, "is to put man's distinctly modern feeling of 'exile,' of abandonment, directly at the center of his stage".[137]

The modernity of Melville is an aspect on which many commentators like to dwell, and indeed, while Whitman could scarcely appear in our age, Melville seems to stand right in the middle. It would be erroneous, however, to believe that his concern is mainly with the fate of the United States, and that his writings somehow foreshadow the disaster of her innocence. To be sure, the American Captain Delano in *Benito Cereno* is innocently blind to what goes on in the Spanish ship which he visits, and in the *Confidence Man* Melville produces a satire on the fallacies of American life. Similarly in his long epic poem *Clarel* there appears in the fourth book the gloomy figure of Ungar, predicting the doom of America and the 'Dark ages of Democracy', with

> Myriads playing pygmy parts –
> Debased into equality.

But these are isolated and partly inconclusive instances, which do not warrant the assertion that all Melville's works allude to the United States and its possible fate.[138] His distinct concern is with the fate of the individual, not the selfishly conquering, accumulating hero of the industrial expansion, but the self, as awareness. It is not accidental that this same Ungar with his uncomfortable message, calls himself 'a wandering Ishmael from the West'.

In this Melville is far more in concurrence with Whitman than the usual rather easy tendency of contrasting the two authors, allows. Definitely, Whitman is more 'nationalistic', yet by no means as 'optimistic' as we are so persistently made to believe.[139] He resembles Melville in his dialectic spirit of contraries. We shall, indeed, always be wrong if we assign to him the position of a single-minded believer in American democracy.[140] In *Democratic Vistas* the childlike faith in the future is

---

[137] *Ibid.*

[138] As does James E. Miller, Jr., *A Reader's Guide to Herman Melville* (New York, 1962), 240, 241. Cf. also Marius Bewley, "Melville and the Democratic Experience", in *Melville: a Collection of Critical Essays*, Richard Chase, ed. (Englwood Cliffs, 1964), 91-116.

[139] For instance Carleton Noyes, *An Approach to Walt Whitman* (Boston, 1910), 177.

[140] About Whitman's 'agonistic' nature see Richard Chase, "Walt Whitman as America's Spokesman", *Whitman: a Collection of Critical Essays*, R. H. Pearce, ed. (Englewood Cliffs, 1962), 161.

contrasted by strong doubts about the contemporary state of the commonwealth. Because his style is less subtle than that of either Emerson or Thoreau, his criticism of the age actually sounds harsher than theirs. He thinks it high time that we diagnosed the disease of the time, and concludes that there has never been more 'hollowness at heart' than at present.[141] He analyzes at length the many aspects of New World life which to him make an appalling spectacle of "corruption, bribery, falsehood, mal-administration". "I say that our New World democracy, however great a success in uplifting the masses out of their sloughs, in materialistic development, products, and in a certain highly-deceptive superficial popular intellectuality, is, so far, an almost complete failure in its social aspects, and in really grand religious, moral, literary and esthetic results." [142]

The clear fact which emerges here is that Whitman, like Melville and the other Transcendentalists, founds his convictions on the autonomy of the individual, the Soul, as he puts it. His belief in democracy is radically contrasted to the mechanical conformist trend which the twentieth-century governing system is to become. For this reason he predicts that democracy will fail, if it does not go deeper than political organization, suffrage and legislation, and produce a great literature as its justification.[143] Whitman here points to the gnawing awareness at that time of separation between the freedom of opportunity (already achieved) and the freedom of culture (more and more elusive). This flows from the recognition of living in a time of crisis, one which is primarily of a cultural nature.[144]

Melville and Whitman, as true Transcendentalists, are deeply involved in the Self-search, the historical nineteenth-century Self-consciousness, which with deliberate persistency sets the world of objects over against the world of awareness. They thus anticipate the self-doubt which in the United States is to become general during the last decade of that century. This development, however, is as far as one can see not stirred up by the Transcendentalist Movement. The American Renaissance is unique. It does not develop. It leaves no school. While the theories of Hegel, Darwin, Kierkegaard, Marx, Comte, Nietzsche evolve, and reach the twentieth century in new varieties, the Transcendentalists have no followers in later decades.

---

[141] W. Whitman, *Complete Writings* (New York, 1902), V, 61.
[142] *Ibid.*, 63.
[143] *Ibid.*, 55 ff.
[144] C. R. Metzger, *Thoreau and Whitman* (Seattle, 1961), 55.

The reasons are probably complicated and cannot here be satisfactorily analyzed. Would it be too audacious to conjecture that inasmuch as they live in a country where cultural estrangement emerges faster and more completely than elsewhere, their admonitions in a prolonged fight would soon seem naive and unrealistic? Their classical stature is ensured and seems to increase with the years. But the effect of their message in a century of decentralized material pursuits must obviously be negative. They focus their attention on the essential sources of life, as they see it. They preach essentials. Theodore Parker calls them the 'first principles', which he deems dangerously lacking in the development of American democracy. "When that great defect – lack of first principles – is corrected, our intensity of life, with the hope and confidence it inspires, will do a great work for us." [145] Now, more than a century later, the idea of first principles has become an abandoned illusion of the social arrangement of pragmatic expediencies.

5. ESCHATOLOGICAL OVERTONES

During the nineteenth century three characteristic trends develop which, though related to each other, yet appear and evolve as distinct entities. The emergence of the *Zeitkritik*, of the tendency toward pessimism, with its connotations of *spleen* and *Weltschmerz*, and of cultural eschatology probably have the same sociological roots, but they manifest themselves in different ways. The social criticism as it appears for instance with Schiller and Fichte, is not necessarily of a despondent nature; it can, on the contrary, predicate a firm belief in progress. Nor can one say that Hegel's thought as a whole conveys gloom, although he himself considers it a confirmation of an end-phase in history.

Eschatology by its very Greek name indicates that the nineteenth century holds no monopoly of this kind of historical speculation. Throughout history there have been prophets fulminating against sacerdotal and governmental systems, while forecasting imminent disaster. Whereas they traditionally confine themselves to a national system, after the revelations of John the Divine the entire world may be marked for doom. The idea of decline and fall, as cultivated by nineteenth-century thinkers, however, is not religiously motivated. With the ex-

---

[145]   Theodore Parker, "The Political Destination of America". Perry Miller, *The American Transcendentalists* (Garden City, N.Y., 1957), 364.

ception of such chiliastic movements as represented for instance by the Jehovah's Witnesses, it is a predominantly cultural concern.

In the center of this eschatological development stands Oswald Spengler whose decline analysis is no mere accidental part of his work, but almost his exclusive lifetime interest. He stands at the center, because no other work of a similar purpose has had such a historic and emotional impact on the intellectual life of the twentieth century as his *Untergang des Abendlandes*. This is not simply explained by the great force of his imagination (resulting as much in grandiose insights as in formidable errors), or the enthralment of his poetic style. This work, written during the first World War, appears timely when the Western mind in general is awakened to the threat of cultural disaster. It has been called the symbol and synthesis of our age, and 'the nearest thing we have to a key to our times".[146] Spengler stands also in the center inasmuch as he represents the crest of a wave, so to speak, in the development of eschatological thinking. After him other works of this nature seem to be continuously stirring reverberations, from Ricarda Huch's *Entpersönlichung* (1922),[147] Toynbee's *Study of History*, to Sorokin's *The Crisis of our Age* and even more recent statements. The individual analyses before him are our concern at this point.

It is not important for us to agree or disagree with cyclical theories, or to assess to what extent Spengler and his predecessors are correct or erroneous in their judgments. The eschatological idea itself has become a fact and factor. As such it cannot be ignored in the description of the development of cultural change, especially since in itself it is a clear expression of estrangement: It is rooted in man's self-conscious asking about the meaning of his time. Whereas the Renaissance man is primarily concerned about his place in the spatial order, in the nineteenth century man wonders about his place in history. Instead of feeling himself at home in his age, he is home-sick. He begins to believe, rightly or wrongly, that his culture is evolving away from the center of life, is growing old, as if it were a biological entity like man himself. Again, that this identification of man's ages with cultural growth can not be verified is immaterial here. The fact that this way of thinking becomes a historical factor is in itself important to us.

[146]   H. S. Hughes, *Oswald Spengler* (New York, 1952), 164-165.
[147]   Ricarda Huch, *Entpersönlichung* (Leipzig, 1922), 223, describes what are to her the signs of decline: the comfortable accommodation with science, the increased governmental machinery, preference for systems, flirtations with Buddhism and Nirvana, occultism, importance of party politics, squeamishness of our feelings, etc.

Cyclical theories about the history of mankind are old. The conception of the Yang and Yin, and the Buddhist Wheel of Becoming are only a few indications of the fact that the first religious and historical thinking concentrates on the cyclical return of seasons and ages.[148] The idea of the Eternal Recurrence is as important for the Stoa as it is for Ibn Khaldun (1332-1406), the Arabian historian who conceives the course of history in waves of rise and fall. He is followed in this by Giambattista Vico, who divides history in three stages: the age of the Gods (divine rule), the age of the Heroes (aristocracy), and the age of Men (democracy and monarchy). His work *The New Science* concludes that when the popular states become corrupt the philosophies decline into scepticism. He proceeds by describing how Providence tries to bring the people back to piety and faith. When religion is lost, according to Vico, there is nothing left to keep society together.[149]

The speculation on history becomes more specific and subjective in the nineteenth century when man is seen by some as having arrived in a historical end-phase. These reflections begin and develop mainly in Germany, with Kierkegaard and Burckhardt standing at the geographic periphery. Why this should be such a predominantly Germanic concern can be left aside. But it is hard to ignore the fact that this preoccupation with culture and cultural decline runs parallel with the new theories on alienation, play and labor. It seems as if there is a hidden relationship which binds these new fields of awareness in a consciousness of history, which again finds its major concentration in German philosophies of history.

It is not surprising then that Hegel's remarkable consciousness of history leads him to the analysis of alienation as well as of cultural decline. In his system, however, the cyclical development is absent. Instead of being based on the biological process of seasons, it views history as an unfolding of three successive periods, each exceeding the previous one in increased freedom. In the last period, when the liberty for all is realized, history arrives in its end-phase, and the philosopher now can describe and analyze the world in conceptional forms. Philosophy, as thought, Hegel believes, enters when actuality has been completed and the developmental process is finished. The philosopher now depicts 'grey-in-grey' an existence which has grown old. He cannot rejuvenate this life, but he can try to understand it. Hegel concludes this observation with

---

[148]   H. Schaller, *Die Europäische Kulturphilosophie* (München, 1940), 5.
[149]   G. Vico, "Principi di una scienze nuova", *Opere* (Milano, 1836), IV, 325 f.

the much-quoted phrase "The owl of Minerva begins its flight when the dusk is falling." [150] Thus in all the many fields which Hegel attempts to probe philosophically, the final chord of real achievement has struck. In literature everything has been said, religion has lost the living element of faith, and according to Löwith, Hegel's philosophy of government is the "recognition of a completed world".[151]

In the work of Karl Friedrich Vollgraff, the earliest forerunner of Spengler, one can find the full cyclical descriptions of civilizations and what happens when they enter the period of senescence. There is no doubt in Vollgraff's mind as to the similarity between the development of the individual and mankind in general. In a broadly based, three-volume work, appearing in 1851, he gives a 'genetic natural history of civil society' in a curious mixture of physical and metaphysical approaches. The history of nations is divided into a healthy, normal phase, and a diseased, abnormal one. The decline of a nation is evident in the fact that individuals direct themselves more exclusively toward physical comfort, which is allied with a desire for luxury. This weakening of man's inner resistance combined with moral laxity, changes the simple urge for subsistence into egotism. It is the beginning of the dissolution, as old age is the beginning of death.[152] It is this egotism that corrupts the roots of civilization.[153] It demonstrates the lack of interest in the values of the good, true and beautiful, and moreover of a susceptibility to religious stirrings. Man in this stage makes only an outward gesture (*affectiert*) of ethics, philosophy, esthetics, and religion.[154] He does not really participate in their essential problems. Affectation as a pseudo-life becomes the criterion. Turning to specific weaknesses, Vollgraff subsequently points to the characteristic trend of critical commentaries on past philosophers, instead of the production of original thought. Similarly, the arts from architecture to poetry live off the fruits of the past and concentrate on merely outward forms, while religion becomes the worship of dead formulas and statutes, easily adapted into a *Staatsreligion*.[155]

Vollgraff sees these general symptoms of degeneration and senescence

---

[150]   Hegel, *op. cit.*, VI, 17.
[151]   "Eine fertig gewordene Welt". Löwith, *op. cit.*, 58.
[152]   K. Vollgraff, *Erster Versuch einer Begründung ... der allgemeinen Ethnologie ...* (Marburg, 1851), 278.
[153]   *Ibid.*, 279.
[154]   *Ibid.*, 281.
[155]   *Ibid.*, 285.

in his own time,[156] and he refers to Niebuhr who, at the outset of the revolution of 1830, wonders if this is the beginning of a period similar to the middle of the third century.[157] But revolutions, Vollgraff adds, are only outward signals of inner decay, which fundamentally is a process of moral weakening. The atrophy of nations is nothing but the decline of that by which mankind distinguishes itself from the bestial, namely its 'feelings of humanity'. the fall of cultures thus lies in the process of gradual dehumanization.

It is clear that this kind of reasoning must easily invite critical questions. One could for instance wonder if the moral level of the nineteenth century is really so far below that of previous periods and ask in what manner this is to be measured. And luxury? Can one maintain that nineteenth-century Vienna is more indulgent and comfort loving than say, fifteenth-century Florence or seventeenth-century Amsterdam? Vollgraff's statements, being without careful qualifications, make themselves immediate targets for attack. Be this as it may, they also reveal, indirectly, a mind busy with the growing urgency of the mechanization and alienation of human actions.

Following Vollgraff's lead, and definitely influenced by his work, Ernst von Lasaulx continues the degeneration theory of culture. The parellel between man and people in their physiological and historical development again is pivotal, and the decline of Ancient Rome and Greece the pattern for our age. Today the stars in the cycle of events stand in the same position as then, and modern man stands "at the evening of a similar catastrophe of European life as that of the fourth century".[158]

Nations are destined to die as much as individuals, and Lasaulx, in contrast to Gobineau, believes this to be so even if the people do not mix with foreign elements.[159] He describes the various symptoms which point to an "invisible, central cause of an inner fatigue in the national energy during the old age of peoples".[160] A general feeling of despondency, doubt, and frustration permeates life, and just as after the time of Aristotle, Sensualist, Skeptic, and Materialist systems emerge. The enfeeblement of moral resistance is evident in the loosening of conjugal

---

[156] *Ibid.*, II, 956 ff.
[157] *Ibid.*, II, 959.
[158] Lasaulx, *Der Untergang des Hellenismus* (München, 1854), 4.
[159] Lasaulx, *Neuer Versuch einer alten ... Philosophie der Geschichte* (München, 1856), 147.
[160] *Ibid.*, 149.

bonds whereby "the foundation of bourgeois life is undermined".[161]
Jurisprudence, far from being the property of the people, becomes a
legalistic affair for lawyers only, and the arts and sciences both suffer
from an intellectualism which prevents original greatness. For greatness
is a matter of character and a feeling of organic fullness which, according to Lasaulx, are now absent.

The general demonstration here is far less detailed than in Vollgraff's
work, but the line of thought is very much the same. Except that Lasaulx'
analysis is in many instances unfortunately dependent on reactionary
views such as those of the Maistre, Görres, and Baader. One continually
senses the persistent ignoring of the progressive and productive forces
which in the successive revolutions of that age give new impetus to
important opportunities of a material and intellectual nature. Lasaulx'
favorite notion is that of a vital energy which generates and drives
national cultures. But it seems a gross injustice to deny to both Europe
and the United States great reservoirs of cultural energy in the middle
of the nineteenth century. To recognize this is not merely a matter of
hindsight. It must have been evident to the many witnessing the new
products of art, literature and science in Lasaulx' time.

Although Lasaulx' analysis thus suffers from a lack of qualifying
judgment and biased historical approach, he is nevertheless important
as a link between Vollgraff and Burckhardt. The significance of Burckhardt in the development of cultural pessimism lies partly in the fact
that his diagnosis of decline is not derived from metaphysical speculations, but from the discipline of history. Burckhardt is responsible for
bringing Lasaulx out of obscurity, and the partial affinity between the
two is undeniable.[162] The fourth chapter of Burckhardt's *Reflections on
History*, with its penetrating analysis of historical crisis, is directly inspired by Lasaulx. But Burckhardt with his far greater factual knowledge, his deeper academic skepticism, never resorts to sweeping judgments, or suffers from emotional bias. On the contrary, his dualistic
outlook, ready to sense the polarities of history, constitutes one of his
most attractive sides. Unlike Lasaulx, he wisely abstains from a broad
speculation on rise and fall movements. He shows a sharp eye for the
contemporary deficiences. which he assesses as vulgarizations and
destructions of a glorious past, yet the conclusion of his chapter on

---

[161] *Ibid.*, 151.
[162] See for a detailed analysis of similarities and differences between the two,
Alfons Koether, *Ernst von Lasaulx' Geschichtsphilosophie und ihr Einfluss auf
Jakob Burckhardts weltgeschichtliche Betrachtungen* (Münster, 1937), 90-123.

crises leaves the alternatives open: is enlightened optimism to last, or will the present pessimism be vindicated in its thinking that we are in the same situation as the Romans of the fourth century?

This dualistic trait in Burckhardt is characteristic for his whole view of historical continuity. No one can reject more emphatically the idea that the course of history follows a world-plan in Hegel's sense, and that on this basis we can anticipate the future.[163] Yet no historian has with more daring thrust ventured into the future and predicted disaster from the levelling trends of the time. He is a great esthete and connoisseur of the most refined forms of sophisticated culture, yet he preaches that the hope for the future lies in the ascetic man with the courage to abstain and renounce.[164]

In the series of analyses of cultural decline Burckhardt's reflections are of special significance, because they shy away from any biological and physiological analogies. There is in his work no effort to establish man's possible course in the future through cultural morphology and seasonal succession. He remains the historian, always guided by the temporal context. His apprehension about future achievements arises precisely from this acute sense of history. If in history it has been established time and again that the individuals and the minority of individuals shape the events and contours of culture,[165] then it is worrying to see that our time is characterized by the trend of sacrificing individuality for the group, the original for the conforming. Clearly we are in the climate of thinking that is typical for Kierkegaard, Nietzsche and the American Transcendentalists as well. Burckhardt in his letters never tires of predicting that pandering to the collective must ultimately result in military dictatorship, since the alternatives of complete democracy and a 'right-less' despotism approach each other in the power of the masses.[166]

Burckhardt dies in 1897, but the fascination with cultural eschatology in Germany continues until Spengler and beyond. It is not necessary to analyze here in full for instance the distinct *Zeitalter* which Lamprecht recognizes in civilizations, the corruption of the ancient world on which Eduard Meyer in *Kleine Schriften* bases his decline theory, or Kurt Breysig's morphology of culture, in order to establish the fact of a new

[163] Burckhardt, *Weltgeschichtliche Betrachtungen* (Frankfurt a/M, n.d.), 8.
[164] K. Löwith, *Meaning in History* (Chicago, 1949), 27.
[165] In the fifth chapter of *Weltgeschichtliche Betrachtungen:* "Das Individuum und das Allgemeine".
[166] Burckhardt to Preen, April 13, 1882.

cultural thinking. Although this is, as said, originally part and parcel of a Germanic mentality, in the twentieth century it spreads to other nations, and is promoted seriously even by those who, as Huizinga for instance, reject Spengler's metaphoric type of reasoning. Already in the previous century the field is not entirely left to the Germanic mind. Flaubert and Gustave le Bon in France, or Brooks and Henry Adams in the United States are fair representatives of cultural pessimism, while Flinders Petrie, in England (although *The Revolutions of Civilization* appears in 1911), is also basically a man of the nineteenth century.

The pessimism of Flaubert in his novels as well as letters strikes us primarily as related to the *spleen* so fashionable among writers of that age, and which one connects with Leopardi, Heine, Lenau, Schopenhauer, Baudelaire, Verlaine. This aspect is not relevant here. But Flaubert in his *Correspondance*, and we may add in his satirical novel *Bouvard et Pécuchet*, not only reveals disillusionment in man (which is a subjective evaluation), but also a judgment on the declining times (which is of a historical nature). Frightened by the revolutionary outbursts in France and elsewhere, he withdraws into a shell in order to safeguard himself from the mob. He sets himself up against all forms of power, be it republican, reactionary, red, blue, or tricolor.[167] In *Bouvard et Pécuchet* he turns as much against the conservative spirit as against the French socialists. In his youth an admirer of the French Revolution, he later becomes disillusioned upon discovering the cruelty and injustices which it entails. To Flaubert there is no *moi collectif*, and he looks at the right to vote with the same contempt as Thoreau. "The fetishism of universal suffrage is as appalling to Flaubert as the infallibility of the pope." [168] In a letter to George Sand he declares that "politics is as dead as theology".[169]

Flaubert's seclusion from the crowd is not unlike that of Burckhardt's, and in other respects also one is inclined to see similarities between the two. But whereas Burckhardt comes to his conclusions through historical data and inferences, Flaubert arrives at his point of view as an artist, who senses the power of conformity conspiring against spontaneous life. The masses are the threat to civilization. To Turgenev he writes: "The bourgeoisie is so dumbfounded that it has no sense left to defend itself, and that which will succeed it is even worse. I feel as sad as a Roman patrician of the fourth century. I feel an irremediable bar-

---

[167]   H. Frejlich, *Flaubert d'après sa correspondance* (Paris, 1933), 244.
[168]   *Ibid.*, 243.
[169]   Flaubert to G. Sand, beginning of June 1869.

THOUGHT ABOUT CULTURAL ESTRANGEMENT

barism rising from below. ... Never before have spiritual interests counted for less. Never has the hatred of greatness, the contempt for beauty, the execration of literature been so manifest. I have always tried to live in an ivory tower, but a tidewave of filth pounds on the walls making them crumble." [170] Flaubert is no despiser of the workers; he makes the distinction between a social class and the formation of a uniform herd which is to terrify culture.

Similar views, but scientifically rather than esthetically developed, appear in Gustave le Bon's *Psychologie des foules* (1895), which describes the role of the masses in the destruction of civilization. Great periods in history according to le Bon are always led by small élite groups, and when they are overpowered by the majority, the dissolution sets in. He follows the familiar analogy of successive ages, believing that when a culture has reached senescence, it will inevitably show a loss of idealism. With the disappearance of its ideal, the people "gradually lose their cohesion, their unity and their vigor ... It is then that the people, divided by their interest and aspirations, and not knowing how to rule themselves, demand to be directed in their most simple acts, and that the central government exercises an absorbing influence. ... With the definite loss of the old ideal the nation ends up by also losing its character. It is nothing but a dust of isolated individuals ... The cycle of national life is a passage from barbarism to civilization during which it pursues a dream, and a dying the moment this dream has lost its force." [171] Thus the conclusion of the work.

Henry Adams is familiar with Le Bon's work, and in *The Degradation of the Democratic Dogma* he quotes from *La psychologie politique*: "The surest symptom of the decadence threatening us is the general enfeeblement of characters ... If we try to discover why so many nations perished after a long decline – why Rome, formerly queen of the world, ended by falling under the barbarian's yoke, we find that these profound falls had generally the same cause – enfeeblement of the Will ... It was always by this enfeeblement of character, and not by that of intelligence that the great peoples disappeared from history." [172] Henry Adams is especially partial to this way of reasoning since it comes from a scientist, and science to him represents the major guide to the historical process. Thus the second law of dynamics, which states that the

[170]   Flaubert to Turgenev, Nov. 13, 1872.
[171]   G. le Bon, *Psychologie des Foules* (Paris, 1925), 31st ed., 178-180.
[172]   H. Adams, *The Degeneration of the Democratic Dogma* (New York, 1958), 249.

material world tends to a dissipation of energy, plays a decisive role in *The Degradation of the Democratic Dogma*. It is connected, as one knows with the law of Entropy, a highly complex and abstract conception for the scientist, but to the vulgar and ignorant historian, as Adams puts it, it "means only that the ash-heap is constantly increasing in size".[173] History, on this basis, is not a science of statistics, but one of vital energy in relation to time.[174] It is a "record of successive phases of contraction divided by periods of explosion".[175] The theory of rise and fall of cultures is not popular with Henry Adams; instead he believes the idea of expansion and contraction to be more scientific, thereby following Goethe's example of the systole and diastole. Over against the fairly optimistic evolutionist doctrine, he adheres to the law of degradation of energy, which he, without questioning the validity of the transition, applies to history: "As an organization society has always been peculiarly subject to degradation of energy, and alike the historians and the physicists invariably stretch Kelvin's law over all organical matter whatever." [176]

Henry's brother Brooks, less inclined to rely on scientific laws, is far more specific and emphatic in predictions of doom. In his introduction to Henry's *Degradation* he insists that the decadence of democracy is caused by the administration of the average. "The democratic principle of public conduct has always been that 'to the victor belongs the spoil,' and public property has been administered accordingly. It is the system of averages and levelling downward." [177] Moreover there are the familiar complaints about the feminist movement, and the undermining of sound family life which threatens the cohesion of the entire social structure. Brooks Adams, anticipating his brother's pessimistic outlook, already in 1896 publishes a cultural critique *The Law of Civilization and Decay*. The core of this work, according to Charles Beard, who has written an introduction to it, is that "fear yields to greed and the economic organization tends to supersede the emotional and martial".

This thesis is derived, partially, from the comparison of cultural patterns, in this case the analogy with the collapse of the Roman empire, which the author puts before us as a warning sign of our own withering

[173]   *Ibid.*, 138.
[174]   *Ibid.*, 203.
[175]   *Ibid.*, 209.
[176]   *Ibid.*, 256.
[177]   *Ibid.*, 121.

vitality. To illustrate the classical tendency to decline, Brooks Adams contrasts Roman art as fake compared to Greek art, which he thinks to be functional. In Greece, a temple apparently of marble, is of marble. A colonnade apparently supporting a portico, does support it. "In Rome the gaudy exterior has nothing whatever to do with the building . . . From the Greek standpoint nothing could be falser, more insulting to the intelligence, or, in a word, more plutocratic." [178]

Plutocratic is one of the key-notions in Brooks Adams' thinking. When greed and monetary power are the ruling determinants of a society the end is inevitable. To find this kind of cultural evaluation in the United States is the more remarkable since, certainly in the nineteenth century, the prevailing mood is one of undaunted optimism. Even if one allows for the doubts and discomforts which begin to show up in the American mind at the time of the Adamses, the daring challenge of involving the supposedly young, buoyant America in an end-phase of history, is an astonishing feat, which gives them a unique place in American historiography.

A final word in this brief survey of cultural pessimism must be devoted to W. M. Flinders Petrie and his *The Revolutions of Civilization*, which is the last conspicuous work in this field before Spengler's entrance. Petrie draws conveniently from his expert knowledge of ancient culture, in order to set up a series of eight periods which succeed each other in fairly regular cultural revolutions. Thus the seventh period runs from about 1200 B.C. to 450 A.D., the eighth from 450-1900. In each of these broad eras, including various national civilizations such as the Egyptian, Cretan, Greek, Etruscan, Roman, European, the pattern shows among other things, how in each culture the turning points in the specific fields of cultural expression occur in a certain order. Sculpture is the first to finish its historical role, then painting, then literature, and after this the final two centuries or so are left to mechanics, science, and wealth, until all signs of importance have vanished.[179] In the later periods we may find great conquerors emerge between the declining phase of literature and technology (mechanics). Thus Ramses II, Caesar, and Napoleon appear at these typical junctures, in the sixth, seventh, and eighth periods of Petrie's World history.

The *Revolutions of Civilization* is clearly based on the rise and fall assumption, and it starts with pointing out that the Etruscans already speak of the Great Year as the period for each nation to flourish and decay

---

[178] B. Adams, *The Law of Civilization and Decay* (New York, 1955), 300.
[179] W. M. F. Petrie, *The Revolutions of Civilization* (London, 1911), 101.

according to the seasons of summer and winter.[180] While in this Petrie differs from the Adamses, in another respect he shows a close affinity. The development of democracy, he holds, is immediately related to the power of wealth. During the unfolding of democratic liberties (which incidentally, coincide with the great phase of literature), the accumulated capital continues to increase. But "when democracy has attained full power, the majority without capital necessarily eat up the capital of the minority, and the civilization steadily decays, until the inferior population is swept away to make room for a fitter people." [181]

An examination of the various theories of cultural decline during the nineteenth century raises the question why such distinguished scholars and authors should arrive at their negative conculsions, in an age so patently full of zest. The nineteenth century IS a period of energy and enterprise. No one can ignore the signs. There is expansion. There is conquering imperialism, conquering Western frontier, conquering science. A new heroic ideal is born in the bourgeois mind. There is Balzac and there is Ibsen. The concert hall is a new cultural event. There is Brahms, Berlioz, Tschaikovsky. The bourgeois produces his own brand of art. What could testify more to vitality than the works of Turner, Renoir, Manet, Monet, Hodler, Cézanne? What could more express confidence than Railroad, Crystal Palace, Eiffel Tower, Sacré Cœur, the *Kaiserreich* of 1871, or Carnegie's *Gospel of Wealth*? Vollgraff, Burckhardt, Petrie and other culture critics must have realized the busy energy around them. Why then their insistent prophecies of doom and decay? Why this complaint about the declining will, character and vitality?

The answer must be sought in their works. They are of course fully aware of the sprawling expansion and nervous dynamism which characterizes the age in many countries. Indeed they do not ignore the new social energy. They simply believe that it is an external energy, dealing with quantity of success rather than quality, directed towards the largest possible vulgarization, leveling, plutocracy. Since to them the individual is equated with quality, the decline of character, that is integrated, harmonious willpower, leads to a diminishing of that natural resistance on which culture depends. Petrie, for instance, thinks strife to be an absolute condition for civilization. When nations reach their fullest wealth and freedom of expression, "there is no more strife with

180   *Ibid.*, 9-10.
181   *Ibid.*, 124.

difficulties and uncertainties of mode; then, strife being ended, decay sets in shortly after".[182]

These views, which are as replete with questionable speculations as of profoundly stirring insights, place the culture critics of the nineteenth century in opposition to the mainstream of the popular activities and beliefs at that time. They are strikingly estranged from their social environment, in the sense that Emerson, Melville and Thoreau are from their community. If we take Henry Adams as a fair representative, the physical movements of his life show a restless flight away from his native soil, to Japan, the South Seas, Egypt, Greece, Sicily, which is in total agreement with his attitude towards modern civilization. So is his intellectual refuge in the world of the twelfth century.

We all probably, in varying degree, have reservations about the formulations, conclusions and predictions of these theorists of decline, especially inasmuch as they refer to our own age, which we naturally hate to accept as one of decadence. Yet there is no denying that their work has had a strong impact on our thinking. They are close to us. What H. S. Commager says about Henry Adams can be said of them all: "We share his doubts and misgivings, his disappointments and frustrations, his sense of failure and of defeat. And we share his fears, we share his longings for the security of a past that is irrevocable." [183] What is fundamentally at stake here is not a matter of rational agreement, but an empathy, an inner relationship of life itself, which includes decay as well as growth.

---

[182]   *Ibid.*, 126.
[183]   H. S. Commager, "Successful Failure", *New York Times Book Review* (Nov. 29, 1964).

CONCLUSION

We have seen that that profound experience which has acquired popular glamor under the name of alienation is not an accidental attribute, but a universal concept. It is universal inasmuch as it appears to be inherently human. When one speaks of cultural alienation, one concentrates on the emergence and subsequent development of this human experience as it becomes a factor in history. The increasing interest of the nineteenth century in culture, cultural history, eschatological speculation, play, labor, and the antagonism between individual and collective, discussed in the preceding pages, is indicative of a new consciousness. This consciousness is collective. It belongs to society as a whole and becomes part of the physiognomy of the last two centuries. The best minds of the period, those usually studied in intellectual history, are the natural representatives of this new and universal awareness. They are the first to register it, and are the most capable of formulating its nature in precise language. Such pivotal figures as Hegel, Goethe, Kierkegaard, Burckhardt, Marx, Nietzsche, Emerson, Thoreau or Melville are in a specific sense ambassadors of a universal consciousness.

Clearly the problems of estrangement do not originate in social wrongs or injustices. There is no point in looking for scapegoats: alienation is not caused by capitalists, socialists, Jews, fascists or communists. Nor will social remedies help to alleviate the burden of the consciousness of alienation. The historian can do no more than describe and analyze remarkable changes in human thinking. These changes, in this case, as we should not tire of repeating to ourselves, are chiefly a matter of consciousness. They are, what is even more important, the results of a developing self-consciousness.

There are two kinds of self-consciousness which can be applied equally well to individual behavior and to collective cultural expressions. The first kind is a technical determination, used especially by Hegel, and extremely pertinent to the historical development of his time.

The second is used colloquially, indicating an awkward embarrassment caused by consciousness of oneself, as Webster tells us. But whereas Hegel's notion conveys a clear attitude of confidence, the common meaning of self-consciousness obviously expresses shy and timid behavior. In both cases, however, the word implies a characteristic split in the functioning of man's mind. Hegel means by self-consciousness a reflection of the spirit on itself, a highly complex activity in the realm of detached reasoning. It includes not only awareness of oneself, but also an awareness of the self-consciousness of others.[1] The common usage of the word self-consciousness could psychologically be analyzed as a reflection on one's actions from the point of view of others, whereby two kinds of consciousness, a subjective and an objective, seem to frustrate each other, resulting in awkward behavior.

Both usages of the notion of self-consciousness, it would appear, are immediately appropriate to the nature of human estrangement, especially when treated in the context of historical and cultural continuity. From the argument of this study, it must be concluded that cultural alienation is a maturing awareness which is able to relate subjective experience to outside reactions in a detached manner. Yet in the process it reveals a marked frustration in the way in which it reflects on cultural achievements. Modern society has exchanged the classical spontaneity of self-expression for deliberate administered forms of education, art, literature, philosophy and religion. For every gain in wisdom and self-control, there is a proportionate loss of youthful creativity.

This gradual change from a spontaneous to an administrative culture does not here have to be illustrated in full. Anyone can easily see how the anxious concern of the average American to HAVE culture at all costs and to construct cultural centers in the most unlikely locations is symptomatic. The emergence of artistic manifestoes since the Romantic movement shows with increased vehemence in the twentieth century that the artist's mind is thoroughly self-conscious about the historical place of his work. Similarly, the modern dominance of the college professor over the 'disciplines' of art, music and drama, the new function of the philosopher as an academic commentator and clarifier, rather than an originator, and the growing importance of official prizes, awards and governmental acknowledgement of the 'artist' as well as his consequent civilized bourgeois status in society – they all go to demonstrate how that which originally is a spontaneous individual expression has be-

---

[1] Cf. Walter Kaufmann, *Hegel* (New York, 1965), 152-153.

come institutionalized and adjusted to the administrative routines of a new era.

The self-consciousness of modern estrangement is foremost of an historical nature. Whereas the awakening of the Renaissance man lies chiefly in his concern with the relationship of man and space, at the end of the eighteenth century man becomes more and more interested in his relationship to time, that is, his place in history. Consequently the nineteenth century is the great age of the consciousness of history and the consciousness of culture, which reflects a preoccupation with the problems of age and of aging. Man shows an increasing inclination to preserve, and becomes fascinated with the idea of the MONUMENT. He has entered the era of museums, art festivals and public libraries, the guardians of his 'heritage'. He is a fanatical believer in the 'record' with which he thinks himself able to serve the future, and anticipate history by perpetuating all the futile details of his life and actions.

Thirdly, the consciousness of cultural estrangement would not play such a pre-eminent role had it not been for the unmistakable accompanying quality of historical maturity. The historical self-consciousness of the nineteenth century indeed is part of a universal maturation of Western man. This to the historian is clearly an embarrassing notion, for it indicates an inward factor defying all scientific precision. The historian moreover dislikes the transference of terms plainly belonging to individual development. He is reluctant to see why the physical and psychological growth of human beings should have any relationship to the historical development of whole societies. There is reason for this reluctance. The opposite attitude might well lead to unsound speculations. Yet it is also evident that not only human beings are subject to the biological necessity of ripening, but equally most living organic units. Any human society is undeniably such an organic unit, and there is therefore no reason why one should not treat it in terms of maturation, provided the analogy be carefully handled.

It is self-evident that the mentality which is capable of setting off its own contemporary scene against the past in a fairly detached manner, and which can theoretically separate the vital areas of individual and group, must have arrived at an advanced state of experience and awareness. Analytical inclination and proficiency occur only after a long process of experiencing and learning.

One of the most conspicuous elements in cultural maturation is an unfolding humanism. This clearly is a wide and vague concept, implying among other things a growing confidence as well as interest in man's autonomous achievements. More specifically, it indicates man's growing capacity for looking at himself objectively after having cleared up some of his fears, emotional confusions and superstitions. The Enlightenment claims to be the great force in this movement, but the real liberating break, as one knows, occurs in the Renaissance, with the late Middle Ages already providing valuable preparatory contributions. This increase in human skill centers in man's ability to evaluate himself in relationship to space and environment which he is learning to observe with scientific detachment. His growing interest in science, indeed, is the sure confirmation of the new objective outlook.

By the beginning of the nineteenth century, however, this detachment acquires such decisive importance that man becomes separated from nature. Goethe is one of the first to see, and warn against, the danger of splitting the world of things from the world of man. The antagonism of the 'two cultures' has become apparent. Maturation in the nineteenth century is no longer marked by confident pride, but rather by a self-conscious worry about man. Humanism is still vital, but man's dignity no longer seems enhanced by the objective world. On the contrary, there are signs that the world of 'things' of the many, of the collective, has become a threat to man's individuality.

Hegel, who has a deep insight into the historical importance of his time, tries in a gigantic effort, to bridge the gap between the consciousness of the self and the outer world. In his famous preface to the *Phenomenology of the Spirit* he declares that the truth is the whole,[2] by which he means that truth comprises the subjective as well as the objective point of view. Hegel's penetrating insight is particularly evident in his being the first to contend that the arts and literature of Western Civilization are exhausted (*ausgesagt*). Every thing has been said; the rest is commentary. The daring admission that the contemporary achievements represent an 'end-phase' in history is itself a true expression of maturity. Naturally, not every one will agree with those who after Hegel have accepted the decline of arts and literature as an historical fact. But the mere existence of this problem or controversy throws a new light on modern history. The possibility of an 'end-phase' is itself already indicative of a change of thinking. It reflects the courage of objectivity which leads maturing minds to face harsh and inexorable realities. Polybius, living in a period in many respects not unlike that of Hegel, as early as the second century B.C., is able to see clearly how

---

[2] Hegel, *Sämtliche Werke* (Lasson, ed., 1928), 21.

the Roman society at its strongest point carries the germs of deterioration.[3]

In this sense cultural estrangement represents an advanced stage of consciousness. It reveals that man can face and accept the fact that he is no longer at home in his own world, in the surroundings of his own making. It reveals that man can adjust himself to an existence divorced from a classical center, that he can abandon not merely superstitions, but also common illusions, including the illusion that his society is still able to excel in great art and literature. Maturity lies in seeing the inevitable and the inevitability of cultural estrangement is that man, once proudly and securely embedded in his own surroundings, begins to conceive of his outer world as an alien force, and a threat to the survival of his individuality.

In the next place it is helpful to understand cultural estrangement not as a fixed position, or a certain clearly defined situation, but foremost as a dialectic awareness. Helpful – provided one does not allow oneself to be trapped in the mechanical constructions which are frequently presented as dialectics. The art of dialectics is not a magician's trick of chopping up metaphysical problems into one, two, three subdivisions, and assuming thereby that one has caught a mystery. This would merely reduce reasoning to hocus-pocus. Dialectic formulations indicate a dynamic process; they represent a form of evolution and are invariably connected with something that is vital and organic. Any dialectic method which abandons this dynamic principle is bound to become mere hollow abstraction, precisely the thing that HAS happened by the misuse of thesis-antithesis-synthesis schemes as a mechanical trick.

Hegel, a pure evolutionist, is fully aware of this danger. The dialectic triad, used for the first time explicitly by Fichte, Schelling, and Schiller, soon deteriorates in the hands of careless followers into a meaningless operation. For Hegel, however, the dialectic process results from an inner development of struggle and conflict. The dialectic nature of the consciousness of alienation is clearly described in the *Phenomenology of the Spirit*. In the section on the self-alienating spirit,[4] Hegel presents the 'actual Self-consciousness' as transferring itself (*übergehen*) to the 'actual world' and then turning back into itself. By entering thus into the world of objects, the Self objectivates itself, that is, alienates itself from the spirit. This relationship between the subject and the object, sustained by the principle of negation and suspension (*Aufhebung*) is the

---

[3] Polybius, VI, 57.
[4] *Phänomenologie des Geistes*, C (BB), VI, B.

dialectic awareness which, applied to cultural history, has been the chief topic of the previous chapters.

Marx, although limiting himself to a specific socio-political consciousness, follows Hegel in the principle of the dialectic process which in Marx's case centers in the separation of the working class from the product of their labor. No less Hegelian, in spite of his protests, is Kierkegaard. His contention that man is estranged from himself and can only overcome this predicament by a 'leap' into Nothingness is, for all its contradiction of the spirit of Hegel's *Phenomenology*, a true confirmation of the dialectic response. Whatever specific attributes one may want to attach to the awareness of estrangement as an historical factor, it is essentially determined by the movements of dialectic negation.

As such it is logically tied up with the idea of evolution. It grows as an awareness of struggle, a notion so pre-eminently decisive for man's destiny. That which in terms of dialectic logic is the relationship between subject and object, transmuted to the realm of cultural history appears as the antagonism of the individual and the collective. For centuries the progress of human society rested on the mutual negation and reconciliation of the two. In the nineteenth century, however, the two components fall apart as separate entities. From this rift there emerge two basic kinds of theory: one supporting the individual as the savior of man's dignity (Existentialist thought), the other, embracing the collective as the hope for human progress (Socialism). This break of consciousness characterizes the whole dualistic outlook of the nineteenth and twentieth century.

Finally, the sources of cultural estrangement are to be found exclusively in the changed historical consciousness which occurs at the end of the eighteenth century. The political revolutions of that time, the Industrial revolution, and the Romantic revolution all have something to do with this. They are of course, three separate events, rightly treated in the history books as autonomous forces. Yet, since their emergence and impact occur coevally, the question must be asked to what extent these three rebellious and disrupting thrusts are culturally connected. Clearly the answer is wrapped in layers of problems. It would require a thoroughly detailed study, and can obviously not be searched for here. But one may say without undue rashness that behind the political, industrial and artistic changes of the time lies a new intellectual questioning, derived from a new awareness. Just as in Renaissance times the outward appearance of Humanism, Protestant and Catholic Reformation and increased scientific interest represent a gradual cultural maturing, so at the end of the eighteenth and the beginning of the nineteenth century disparate cultural changes point to a single new historic awakening.

We have seen that Schiller, living in this critical period, is the first to analyze the split between the authenticity of man and modern society. It is significant that, although a poet, he bases his reasoning not merely on artistic premises, but also on the realities of both the French revolution and the industrial upheaval. This three-fold response of the human consciousness is clearly revealed in his *Esthetic Letters.* To be sure, in this work the artistic ideas and the reaction to the French revolution play a greater role than the references to the Industrial revolution. Schiller's demonstrations rest on the combination of the artist and the statesman. Yet, as we have noted, in the pivotal passage of the sixth letter, which gives the earliest definition of social estrangement, the problem of labor and mechanization is essential.

Thus, the origins of cultural alienation lie in the consciousness which both brings forth and responds to the French revolution, the Industrial revolution, and the Romantic movement. The very nature of consciousness almost implies inward debate, and indeed in Schiller's mind this debate is clearly demonstrated in at least two of these areas. Originally a champion of the new political liberties, his enthusiasm is soon checked with the rising of the proletarian masses. It is the time of the Bastille and the regicide of 1793. What Schiller knows about the beginning of the socialist movement with the 'conspiracy' of Babeuf in 1796 is not recorded. But while supporting the reasonable demands for political freedom, he tries to resist the incipient trend of mob domination. With regard to the Romantic movement he appears to be equally dualistic.[5] While he exercises a decisive influence on the formation of the early Romantic principles in Germany, he, like Goethe, stays deliberately aloof from the Jena circle and steers clear of their excesses. From the outset of the development of social and cultural estrangement the intellectual cleft, so typical for the whole problem, is patently manifest.

Century after century man works and gets tired, but never questions the relationships between work, tools and man's inner dignity. Nor is the division of labor unknown to him. Only after long social and mental experience does man begin to think about the possibility of a dehumanizing element in labor practices, and the links between product, pro-

---

[5] See my *Freedom and Dignity* (The Hague, 1965), 29 ff.

ducer, commodity value and demand. It is from this new kind of reflection that arises a man like Adam Smith.

Century after century man plays, consciously in hours of relaxation, unconsciously in the AGONAL forms of civilization. But he is rarely concerned with the philosophical implication of play, and it does not occur to him that it is a problem worth reflecting upon. It is only after long experience of creative culture that he is able to detach himself from his own achievements and understand how they appear in the structure of play. It is from this critical detachment that emerges, among other things, an understanding of the *homo ludens* like that of Schiller.

This self-evaluation of man in his social context, shown in the awareness of his labor and play, has, in the previous chapters, also been analyzed in connection with his new concern for culture and history, with the massification of society and the isolation of the individual, as well as with cultural pessimism and eschatological theories. This historical self-evaluation is possible only at a time when man indeed is self-consciously separated from his own environment.

It is the Industrial revolution that makes the leading minds of the period reflect on the nature of play and work. Pestalozzi, the Swiss pedagogue, and contemporary of Schiller, Adam Smith and Hegel, initiates an education immediately relevant to the misery of the factory. In a study of *Popular Education and Industry*, he deplores the routine mechanism of isolated professional skills which he believes harmful to the development of man.[6] Far from being opposed to industrialization, Pestalozzi aims at overcoming the mental isolation of the worker by a rounded popular schooling, which is "actually a means of humanizing industry".[7]

Thus, about a quarter of a century before Marx begins his activities, Pestalozzi has clear ideas about the *Aneignung*, the bringing back of the alienated worker to a humanized society.

It is the French revolution that opens people's eyes to the possibilities of the masses as a political instrument. A *Manifesto of the Equals*, originating in the circle of Babeuf in 1796, views the French revolution merely as a precursor to a far greater one, namely that which is to establish the Republic of Equals. While the Declaration of Human Rights and the Constitution of 1791 still accept property as sacred, the

[6]   Pestalozzi, *Gesammelte Werke* (Zürich, 1946), VII, 441.
[7]   *Ibid.*, VII, 456. Further in the essay on *Industry, Education and Politics* of 1822. Cf. also Bruno Bendokat, *Industriepädagogik bei den Philanthropen und bei Pestalozzi* (Halle, 1933).

Babouvists proclaim the Community of Goods. "No more private property in land: the earth is nobody's. We claim, we will the common use of the fruits of the earth: its fruits are everybody's." [8] Absolute equality also implies one uniform need, opportunity and mental faculty. Thus "let there be for all one education and one standard of life".

More than fifty years before Marx and Engels launch their Communist Manifesto, the Babouvists already proclaim the common republic with common property, products and mental ability. The question which this raises for the individuality of man and its bearing on his cultural progress has been answered by reference to such men as Goethe, Kierkegaard, Flaubert or Burckhardt. But the Babouvists themselves are also well aware of this threat. In the same manifesto they declare: "Perish, if need be, all arts as long as we have real equality!" From now on the mutual enmity between the single and the mass is realized and becomes a factor in history. The relationship between massive conformity and the perishing of the arts figures more and more insistently in critical minds. The growing cultural pessimism with its ensuing eschatological speculation from Hegel to Spengler coincides with the results of the successive egalitarian revolutions.

It is the Romantic revolution that in manifold expressions demonstrates man's fear of constricting conformity. Romanticism has too often been treated according to its accidental attributes. Fundamentally, however, the movement represents a rebellion against the mechanization of form. Instead the Romanticist wants form as a spontaneous manifestation. Individual originality is the key notion to his mind and his work. This sets him squarely against the obvious historical trend. Society around him, at least as he understands it, appears to be in a process of formalization and ossification. It is erroneous to think that the Romanticist is against society. He is merely against the specific contemporary social agreement, which constricts the authenticity of the individual. He therefore seeks a new congenial community. He becomes a wanderer in search of his authentic self.

The Wanderer is the characteristic Romanticist configuration. Shelley's Alastor, Ibsen's Brand, Byron's Childe Harold, Melville's Ishmael, Goethe's Faust, and the more cheerful *Taugenichts* of Eichendorff's imagination are only a few representatives of the mind which has lost its cultural home. He is the *isolato* as Melville presents him in practically all the characters of *Moby Dick*. The Wanderer is the typical nine-

[8]   To be found in *Revolution from 1789-1906*, R. Postgate, ed. (New York, 1962), 55.

teenth-century embodiment of the stranger, who not only has lost his home, but his location in time as well. Hence the appearance of that intellectual tedium, which the French language calls *spleen* and the English *ennui*. The Germans speak of *Weltschmerz*, which is the suffering from one's contemporary world, but which can be more appropriately translated as the suffering from time. The Romanticist's dream is the Golden Age which he conceives of either in the past, or in the future – sometimes in both. He is painfully divorced from the contemporary order. The Romantic revolt, like the political and industrial revolutions of the age, has the effect of leaving man's consciousness isolated amidst the growing complexities of the outside world.

Or, should we not rather say that the Romantic, Industrial and French revolutions are the PRODUCT of the consciousness of estrangement? Instead of viewing the artistic, scientific and egalitarian upheavals at the end of the eighteenth century as opening man's eyes to his isolated situation, should we not rather understand them as outward manifestations, originating in the alienated consciousness of the mind?

If so, this may give at least a partial answer to the question why the three parallel revolutions beginning in the final decade of the eighteenth century, historically have never ended. The Industrial revolution, through ups and downs of intensity, is still with us. Computerized management is merely a new phase in the development which replaces spontaneous human labor with administered machine labor. Similarly the egalitarian revolutions did not end in 1789. Nor in 1796, 1830, 1848, or 1917. From National Assembly and Bastille into our own time, as the proletarian order gradually establishes itself, the influence of mass opinion and conforming consensus proceeds with undiminished impact. Lastly, the Romantic revolution, in spite of important counterthrusts from such varying groups as the Parnassiens, the Naturalists, the Constructivists, to name only a few, has never ceased to revive itself, albeit under different labels. Championing the originality of the individual, it has in the twentieth century re-emerged in the many expressionistic art forms, which with increasingly violent manifestoes have rebelled against what they believe to be the encroachment on the liberty of the artistic imagination. No matter on which side these three revolutions may appear to stand, they are still active and immediately related to the awareness of liberty – and who can foretell the outcome?

The continuousness of the industrial, political and artistic revolutions, then, may well be explained as a reflection of the continuousness of man's cultural isolation. It is misleading and historically false to consider human estrangement as a social aspect of Western civilization after the second World War, and supposedly overcome by the 1960's. It indeed represents a gradual development which, beginning about two hundred years ago, shows a rift in the consciousness of human liberty, still widening at the present time.

Who can foretell the end?

STUDIES IN THE SOCIAL SCIENCES

edited by

C. A. O. van Nieuwenhuijze

1. C. A. O. van Nieuwenhuijze: *The Nation and the Ideal City: Three Studies in Social Identity.* 1966. 148 pp., 14 figs.
ƒ 21,50/$6.15

2. Jelle C. Riemersma: *Religious Factors in Early Dutch Capitalism 1550-1650.* 1967. 98 pp. ƒ 14,—/$4.00

3. C. A. O. van Nieuwenhuijze: *Intelligible Fields in the Social Sciences.* 1967. 285 pp. ƒ 36,—/$10.30

MOUTON · PUBLISHERS · THE HAGUE